A volume in the series

MASTERS of MODERN LANDSCAPE DESIGN

T0364841

LALH

Library of American Landscape History

LAWRENCE HALPRIN

KENNETH I. HELPHAND

THE UNIVERSITY OF GEORGIA PRESS

ATHENS

LIBRARY OF AMERICAN LANDSCAPE HISTORY

AMHERST, MASSACHUSETTS

To the next generation of Helphands
Zoe, Jonah, Selah, and Cyrus

Published by the University of Georgia Press
Athens, Georgia 30602
www.ugapress.org
in association with Library of American Landscape History

© 2017 by Library of American Landscape History
All rights reserved

Designed and typeset by Jonathan D. Lippincott
Set in Bembo

Printed and bound by Four Colour Print Group
The paper in this book meets the guidelines for
permanence and durability of the Committee on
Production Guidelines for Book Longevity of the
Council on Library Resources.

Printed in Korea

17 18 19 20 21 P 5 4 3 2 1

Library of Congress Cataloging-in-Publication Data

Names: Helphand, Kenneth I., author.
Title: Lawrence Halprin / Kenneth I. Helphand.
Description: Athens : The University of Georgia Press ; Amherst,
    Massachusetts : Library of American Landscape History, [2017] |
    Series: Masters of modern landscape design | Includes bibliographical
    references and index.
Identifiers: LCCN 2017012486 | ISBN 9780820352077 (paperback :
    alk. paper)
Subjects: LCSH: Halprin, Lawrence. | Landscape architects—United
    States—Biography.
Classification: LCC SB470.H35 H45 2017 | DDC 712.092 [B] —dc23
    LC record available at https://lccn.loc.gov/2017012486

Frontispiece: Lawrence Halprin. Photograph by Rondal Partridge.
Courtesy Lawrence Halprin Collection, Architectural Archives,
University of Pennsylvania

SERIES FUNDERS

Ann and Clayton Wilhite
Ann Arbor Area Community Foundation

Dede Delaney and James R. Turner
Blackhaw Fund—Impact Assets

Nancy R. Turner
Viburnum Trilobum Fund—New York Community Trust

VOLUME FUNDERS

Hubbard Educational Foundation

Michael and Evelyn Jefcoat

Cynthia Hewitt and Dan Holloway

Anonymous

Foundation for Landscape Studies

Shannon Hackett

CONTENTS

PREFACE

Over the course of his long career, Lawrence Halprin (1916–2009) created some of the best-known urban landscapes of the twentieth century—Portland Open Space Sequence, Ghirardelli Square in San Francisco, Bunker Hill Steps in Los Angeles, and the Franklin Delano Roosevelt Memorial in Washington, DC. In his working methods, Halprin also left a lasting influence on the profession. Approaching design as a multivalent process, he focused on the people and activities that would determine and then animate the urban places he designed. Halprin's commitment to social activism was unswerving, and he was not afraid to experiment on a grand scale. "An optimist and activist, an innovator and instigator, a trailblazer and trendsetter," writes author Kenneth Helphand, "Halprin designed landscapes that reflected and encouraged the democratic and participatory ethic of his era."

During the course of the 1960s, Halprin assembled a large San Francisco firm—in his own immodest view, "the greatest landscape architecture office on earth"—where his improvisatory methods were supported by many talented assistants. As a young man in the office of Thomas Church in the late 1940s, Halprin benefited from a wise mentor, and there is little question that Halprin's staff, too, learned much from their leader as they supported his experimental methods. Larry's wife, Anna Schuman Halprin, an innovative choreographer, was a frequent collaborator from the time of their marriage in 1940, and her influence is evident as well in many aspects of the landscape architect's work, particularly in the development of a graphic technique—"motation"—that captured movement through time and space.

Halprin's legacy seems almost paradoxical. He was among the first to assert a role for landscape architects in revitalizing failed urban places, and he brought to these projects a passion for nature. "The act of transmuting the experience of the natural landscape into human-made experience is, for me, the essence of the art of landscape design," he wrote in 1995. Halprin's most successful designs evoke geological formations on a vast scale and ecological processes that are equally epic. Through these built works, he exuberantly straddled the perceived divide between art and ecology that dominated so much landscape architectural discourse in the late twentieth century, and in doing so offered city dwellers healing—at times, even rapturous—experiences in the urban landscape.

I am grateful to Kenny Helphand for writing this book for the Masters of Modern Landscape Design series and to the team of editors who assisted in the task, especially Sarah Allaback and Carol Betsch, who also created the index. My thanks go to Jonathan Lippincott for the sleek design and to our partners at University of Georgia Press for the fine production. We are also indebted to the Bruce and Georgia

McEver Fund for the Arts and Environment for its support of the series. And we thank the generous donors who made this volume possible, the Hubbard Educational Foundation and the Foundation for Landscape Studies, as well as the Masters of Modern Landscape Design series funders.

Robin Karson
Executive Director
Library of American Landscape History

ACKNOWLEDGMENTS

Many individuals contributed directly or indirectly to the research and creation of this book, as readers, editors, reviewers, fellow scholars, supporters, photographers, and informants. They include those who read the entire or portions of the manuscript, those who shared their experiences working on Halprin projects, and fellow Halprin scholars: Thaisa Way, Kathleen John-Alder, Laurie Olin, Steve Koch, Randy Fong, Deni Ruggeri, Robert Jackson, Ben Helphand, Sam Helphand, Elaine Winik, Robin Karson and Sarah Allaback of the Library of American Landscape History, copy editor Carol Betsch, Judith Wasserman, Alison Hirsch, Ann Komara, Elizabeth Meyer, Randy Hester, David Hulse, Randy Gragg, Reuben Rainey, John Beardsley, Charles Birnbaum, Peter Walker, Donlyn Lyndon, Bruce Levin, Shlomo Aronson. I thank Pieter Van Remoortere, Carol Stafford Ohls, and Emma Froh for their drawings. Bill Whitaker and Nancy Thorne of the Architectural Archives at the University of Pennsylvania were invaluable allies in gathering and selecting the illustrative materials. My greatest debt is to the Halprin family and especially Anna Halprin for sharing her experiences at her home and on the dance deck. I would also like to acknowledge the unsung contributors to this book, the many people I have observed for almost a half century fortunate enough to experience the landscapes designed by Larry Halprin.

My wife Margot accompanied me as I visited, or more often revisited, the sites described in this book. We shared the pleasure of the places and the ideas they embody, and I experienced them through her senses as well as my own.

LAWRENCE HALPRIN

OVERVIEW

On the afternoon of September 14, 2008, a beautiful late summer day in downtown Portland, Oregon, dancers dressed in blue splashed, bathed, and climbed in a grand fountain whose waters cascaded over concrete cliffs. An audience gathered beneath a canopy of trees and joined the performers in a parade, winding its way to a park in which orange-clad dancers and musicians wandered over green mounds. Participants soon discovered another designed landscape, where dancers in yellow and white costumes were balancing on walls and immersing themselves in water. The group continued its procession, encircling and dancing around a small urban spring. This was "The City Dance of Lawrence and Anna Halprin," a choreographed celebration of the fortieth anniversary of Portland's Open Space Sequence, a quartet of public spaces designed by the landscape architect. The Halprins were not in attendance that day, but this public tribute bore witness to the enduring value of a groundbreaking project that is now a civic landmark.[1]

A different type of celebration took place at the dedication of this space on June 23, 1970. The month before, the Kent State shootings had fueled Vietnam War protests at Portland State University, and a violent clash between students and police ensued. The crowd gathered around Forecourt Fountain included those responsible for law enforcement and clusters of students. As tension between the groups began to build, Lawrence Halprin stepped forward and took up the microphone: "These very straight people somehow understand what cities can be all about," he said, gesturing toward the police officers. "I hope this will help us live together as a community both here and all over this planet earth." When the fountain was turned on, its cascade increasing to a flow of 13,000 gallons per minute, the spectacle transformed a potential confrontation into a group celebration. Then Hal-

Fig. 1. Forecourt (Ira Keller) Fountain, Portland, Oregon, 2010. Courtesy Wikimedia Commons.

prin walked into the water, along with many spectators, experiencing the wonder of a "Sierra stream" in the middle of downtown Portland.[2] The occasion represented the fulfillment of his ongoing effort to "create the possibility for events to happen," which he considered "the essential purpose of design."[3] Throughout his career Lawrence Halprin created places for events—both choreographed and spontaneous—and in doing so, his modernist landscape designs enlivened places and enriched the human experience (fig. 1).

All American landscape architects are indebted to Frederick Law Olmsted Sr., often referred to as the founder of the profession, but Halprin has been singled out for embracing the essential aspects of his legacy—the importance of promoting a reform agenda and championing nature as an uplifting moral force through the artistry of landscape design. Like Olmsted, Halprin distinguished himself by engaging in the passions and issues of his time: social activism, environmentalism, and the arts. As a young man he committed himself to the Zionist experiment in Palestine, served during World War II, and venerated Franklin Delano Roosevelt and the ideals of the New Deal.[4] During the 1960s, Halprin and his wife Anna, an innovator in the world of contemporary dance, became immersed in the dramatic cultural and social changes of the era. They cultivated an avant-garde sensibility and explored the human potential movement, environmental psychology, urban revitalization and preservation, environmentalism, and ecology. Halprin's work was in the vanguard of an effort to reimagine the public life of the American city. At the time, New York City parks commissioner Thomas Hoving was establishing policies to begin revitalizing the city's parks; M. Paul Friedberg and Richard Dattner were reconceiving the urban playground; William Whyte undertook his pioneering "Street Life Project"; and Kevin Lynch's *The Image of the City* (1960) and Bernard Rudofsky's *Streets for People* (1969) were published.

Postwar America was the scene of growing affluence, suburbanization, and urban renewal followed by the dramatic cultural and social changes of the 1960s. In this context, Halprin took on the challenging new project types and issues of his day by developing a trailblazing practice that experimented with adaptive reuse and ecological design in relation to suburban shopping malls, the freeway, and revitalization of the urban core. He communicated his work in a variety of venues—lectures, books, exhibits, and occasional teaching—and became a public figure who consulted on important commissions throughout the country. Along with his contemporary Ian McHarg, Halprin was his generation's great promoter and proselytizer for the significance of landscape architecture as environmental design.

The public and private open spaces of the city are the key to understanding much of Halprin's work. His urban sensibility was shaped by his New York childhood, his time in Jerusalem, his base in San Francisco, and his journeys to many of the world's great cities. In his first book, *Cities* (1963), he challenged environmental designers to create places like the destinations they chose to visit, photograph, and sketch. He urged them to design cities that would "provide a creative environment for people to live in." By this he meant cities with great diversity, freedom of choice, and a "maximum of interaction between people and their urban surroundings." To assist designers in achieving these ambitious goals, Halprin conceived of the "RSVP cycles," a methodology intended to encourage personal creativity and collaborative design.

Halprin's interest in the creative process derived in part

from his engagement with Jungian psychology and its attention to the imagery of universal archetypes—concepts introduced to Halprin by his therapist, the Jungian psychologist Joseph L. Henderson, and the Gestalt psychiatrist Fritz Perls. The RSVP cycles exemplified a passion he would explore throughout his career in his lifelong search for "a creative process. A constantly changing sequence where people are the generators, their creative activities are the aim, and the physical elements are the tools."[5] As an artist, Halprin responded to new influences both personal and professional, but Israel, the Sierra Nevada, Sea Ranch, and his Bay Area home remained touchstones—places that he often returned to for inspiration and solace. They fueled his ideas about design, the relationship between humans and the natural world, and the creation of unforgettable landscapes.

Halprin's personal relationship with the land and state of Israel, which lasted almost eighty years, impacted his life's trajectory. He reveled in Jerusalem's history and what he called the "cacophony of life all around" the exotic, pedestrian-friendly city. He constantly drew its walls, streets, markets, ruins, trees, and holy sites. Reflecting later in life on his experiences there, he wrote with nostalgia of how Israel and Jerusalem had influenced his value system. "I have been deeply swayed by Israelis' reverence for the land—the people's profound identification with their ancestors and their past and the almost mystical identification they have with Jerusalem. . . . In this way I have developed an identity with Jerusalem—a commitment to it as a physical manifestation of ethical and moral principles. . . . The ancient city and its bazaars, the winding stony streets and coffee houses are part of my inner consciousness—the landscape of rounded hills and deep black pines—all have become a part of my life choreography"[6] (fig. 2).

march 30- 1979

Fig. 2. Jerusalem, drawing, March 30, 1979. Courtesy Lawrence Halprin Collection, The Architectural Archives, University of Pennsylvania (LHC).

Israel was close to his heart, but the other influential landscapes were closer to home and exemplified a cross section of California, from the rugged Pacific shore to the crests of the Sierra. Both of these sublime landscapes exhibit the power and magnificence of nature. Sea Ranch, the site of a planned private community along the Sonoma County coast, became the locus of Halprin's experiment in ecological design. In researching the project, he exhaustively walked the land and selected a dramatic spot, cradled in a niche overlooking the Pacific, where he built a cabin that he designed with Charles Moore.[7] Over nearly fifty years he returned regularly, obsessively studying and drawing the surrounding landscape in all seasons. His drawings captured Sea Ranch's dramatic changes in topography—from precipitous cliffs to pastoral meadow to great woods. For Halprin, the landscape's dynamic characteristics may have been its most important feature—the ever-changing sea, the shifting flight of birds, the changes in vegetation, the tidal fluctuation.

Two hundred miles to the east of Sea Ranch are the Sierra Nevada. While hiking in this terrain, Halprin discovered what he called "the Gardens of the High Sierra," his title for an article in J. B. Jackson's *Landscape* magazine in 1961.[8] Gardens, he astutely observed, are created by acts of the mind as well as the hand. This early article expresses the germ of an anti-pictorial design approach he called "naturalism." In these "gardens" of the Sierra, Halprin recognized how natural processes had created these places, and he perceived that process and product were interconnected, even "synonymous."[9] He was fascinated by the geology, the qualities of stone, and especially by the streams cascading down from the peaks. In Leonardo-like fashion he not only drew streams but also analyzed them, taking an almost anatomical approach in attempting to understand the interaction of water and stone, the shape and sound of the water, how it felt and looked. In his notebooks he listed the variety of appealing aesthetic qualities of the Sierra: "picturesque, formal, painterly, sounds, landscape, choreographic, composition"—all qualities he tried to introduce into the urban landscape.[10] In this high country he saw how the "powerful yet refined order of nature opened up a vast aesthetic territory that transformed my basic approach to design"[11] (fig. 3).

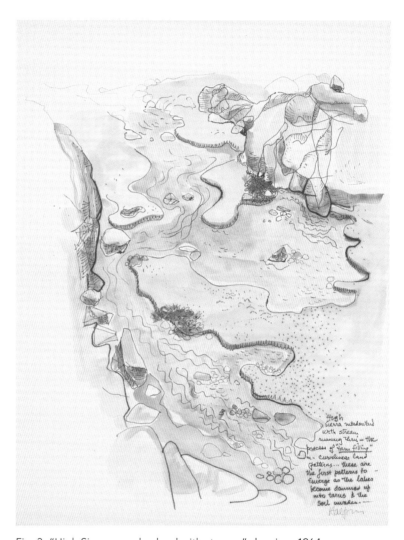

Fig. 3. "High Sierra meadowland with stream," drawing, 1964. Courtesy LHC.

Between the Pacific and the High Sierra was the California landscape that exerted its powerful influence on him daily—the wooded slopes of Mount Tamalpais in Marin County, where he located his home, just over the Golden Gate Bridge from San Francisco, where he had his office for sixty years. This beautiful city is renowned for its combination of urbanity, progressiveness, and dramatic landscape, traits Halprin often sought to achieve in his work. In a sense the contrast between these landscapes, from dense cities to wild places, represented the breadth of his appreciation. Halprin was deeply conscious of the impact of his surroundings, and his prolific notebooks contain drawings and ruminations on the significance of places and experiences. He responded to the western landscape with a rugged, dramatic landscape design vocabulary that was not merely visual, scenic, or pastoral. Even where he employed the more conventional design language of the day he described encounters, the pleasure of moving through spaces and literally climbing into designs. The spirit of his work is enthusiastic and energetic, merging the playful and the profound. The people-oriented landscapes Halprin designed often expressed aspects of his extroverted, charismatic personality.

Halprin was a product of what Tom Brokaw called "the Greatest Generation"—those American men and women who were reared during the Great Depression, served at home and overseas during the Second World War, and helped build the postwar peace. He was ambitious, with exceedingly high standards and no shortage of ego. In his own 1969 diagrammatic history of his firm, Halprin wrote, "Because of design talent and insistence on quality and follow-through [he] achieved the greatest landscape office on earth."[12] Though the claim was hyperbolic, his assessment of the characteristics that made his work so successful was exactly right. An optimist and activist, an innovator and instigator, a trailblazer and trendsetter, Halprin found himself well positioned to design landscapes that reflected and encouraged the democratic and participatory ethic of his era. Later in his career, he would further define his purpose as a landscape architect: "Landscape design *is* about social relevance. It can become poetic and symbolic, but perhaps most importantly, it can articulate a culture's most spiritual values."[13]

Lawrence Halprin, the eldest child of Rose Luria Halprin and Samuel W. Halprin, was born in New York City in 1916. He and his sister Ruth (b. 1924) were raised in Brooklyn, within a deeply committed Zionist family. His mother served two terms as president of Hadassah, the Women's Zionist Organization of America, and his father was a businessman who eventually ran Landseas, an exporting company with connections in Israel.[14] Before the stock market crash, the family spent a year traveling and lived in Jerusalem for several months, during which Halprin celebrated his bar mitzvah. As a teenager, he attended Brooklyn Polytechnic Preparatory Country Day School for Boys, where he excelled in sports and painting. He was privileged enough to attend summer camp at Camp Greylock in the Berkshires, but also participated in the Civilian Conservation Corps. After graduating from high school in 1933, he lived in Israel for two years, working in a factory by the Dead Sea, on a ranch, and in construction. Most important, he joined a group of young people who established Kibbutz Ein Hashofet near Haifa when kibbutzim were still in their pioneering stage. Halprin's time on the kibbutz influenced his life's course, his ethics, and his sense of community.

On returning to the States, Halprin studied plant sciences at Cornell University, earning a bachelor of science degree in 1939. He then enrolled at the University of Wisconsin–Madison to study horticulture, where he met the dancer Anna Schuman (fig. 4). The two married in 1940. Halprin earned his master of science in 1941, but a visit to Taliesin, Frank Lloyd Wright's studio in Spring Green,

Fig. 4. Lawrence and Anna Halprin, 1952. Courtesy Anna Halprin.

Wisconsin, sparked his interest in architecture. He turned to landscape architecture after discovering Christopher Tunnard's *Gardens in the Modern Landscape* (1938), a collection of essays that became one of the most influential texts in the early years of the modernist movement in landscape design. With the assistance of his professors at Wisconsin, Halprin pursued his new interest and received a scholarship to study at Harvard University's Graduate School of Design in 1942. The couple moved to Cambridge, where Anna offered dance classes for design students and lectured on "dance and architecture."

This was only a few years after the school's modern "revolution" had replaced the traditional Beaux-Arts curriculum with a Bauhaus education. Harvard's new faculty included the European refugees Walter Gropius and Marcel Breuer, as well as Tunnard, who had been asked to lecture by students Dan Kiley, Garrett Eckbo, and James Rose and then invited to teach at the GSD. The Bauhaus program in Germany did not include landscape architecture, but its philosophy of interdisciplinary work, transplanted to America, had a profound impact on the profession. Halprin, in particular, benefited from a system that embraced all the arts and emphasized the importance of collaboration. Unlike many of his colleagues who were influenced solely by the formal language of the Bauhaus, Halprin also aspired to its underlying philosophy that design could exert a positive impact on society.

Halprin had intended to return to Palestine after finishing his studies to help build the Jewish state, but World War II interceded, and in December 1943 he left Harvard to enlist in the navy; he was awarded a bachelor degree in landscape architecture the following month. Halprin served in the Pacific as a lieutenant junior grade. During the battle of Okinawa, a kamikaze plane hit his destroyer, the USS

Morris, and he was put on survivor's leave in San Francisco (fig. 5). In 1945, shortly after his discharge from the navy, he obtained a job with the landscape architect Thomas

Fig. 5. "Late afternoon focsle, USS *Morris*, Hollandia," pen and ink drawing, 1943. Courtesy Halprin family.

Church through a recommendation from the architect William Wurster, who had befriended him at Harvard and with whom he would collaborate in later years. San Francisco and its environs—including Marin County, where the Halprins settled—was emerging as a center of design innovation. The city would prove to be Halprin's most significant laboratory and a place on which he made a lasting imprint.

When he entered the Church office, Halprin joined a group of California landscape architects who were particularly attuned to the uniqueness and diversity of the regional landscape. This "California school," which would grow to include Garrett Eckbo, Robert Royston, Doug Baylis, Ted Osmundson, and Geraldine Knight Scott, among others, capitalized on the region's affinity to Mediterranean design and its often-romanticized Spanish and Italian antecedents. Church and the other members of the school felt less bound to classical design and artistic tradition and encouraged active engagement with the landscape in a climate that enabled year-round outdoor activity. Their work appeared on the pages of *Sunset* magazine, popularizing an image of the California "good life" within the reach of middle-class residents.

During his three years in the Church office, Halprin honed his skills in all aspects of design. He benefited from his mentor's Beaux-Arts training, modernist sensibility, and sympathetic response to the particularities of both site and client. His final work with Church, the Donnell garden (also known as El Novillero) in Sonoma, is recognized as one of the landmarks of modern design. This studied composition—with its famous biomorphic swimming pool and live oaks set within the grid of a redwood deck—was a harbinger of things to come for the young landscape architect. In 1949, soon after the completion of the project, Halprin established his own office in San Francisco and hired Jean Walton, a horticulturalist who assumed responsibility for planting design.

The firm of Lawrence Halprin initially focused on residential commissions in the Bay Area, completing close to three hundred in its inaugural decade. Like many young practitioners, Halprin created his first independent designs for family members. In 1949 he had designed a garden for his in-laws in Woodside, south of San Francisco, that preserved half of the four-acre site as a pastoral meadow, included the requisite swimming pool, and united the open spaces with the pool and house with a curvilinear walk. It was the first of Halprin's many collaborations with William Wurster, who had since become dean of architecture at Berkeley (fig. 6).

Halprin received his first public commission, a large-scale landscape plan for the Marin General Hospital in Novato, in 1950 and completed it two years later. Within the confines of a restrictive building program, he created

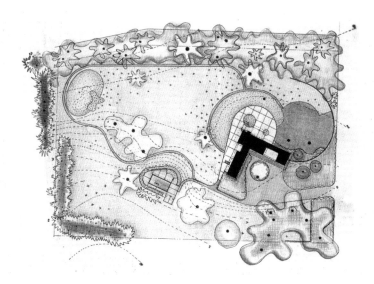

Fig. 6. Schuman garden, Woodside, plan, c. 1949. Courtesy LHC.

intimate spaces that provided people with a respite from the starkness of the medical environment. These included a circular Bar-B-Que Terrace surrounded by palm trees and an Ambulatory Terrace overlooking a marsh. In 1960 he would return to oversee the landscape aspect of the site's expansion.

The Caygill garden (1951) in Orinda, California, exemplified the emerging California lifestyle with a fire pit as the setting for outdoor activity. Halprin's office at the base of Telegraph Hill sported a roof deck, also a feature at the nearby Simon roof garden (1951), where he experimented with a four-foot grid design, modules of redwood decking, raised square planters with bamboo, and a composition of stone and gravel that recalled a dry river—all carefully calibrated to keep the roof load low; a sliding-glass door opened to the garden and views of the Bay Bridge. The Simon roof garden, the first of Halprin's works published internationally, appeared on the July 1953 cover of *Sunset* magazine (fig. 7). Halprin had quickly captured the essence of the regional aesthetic and launched himself into the current design scene.

The character of Halprin's residential design during the first decade of his firm is perhaps best illustrated by the McIntyre garden (1959) in Hillsborough, south of San Francisco in San Mateo County. Set in a clearing within a eucalyptus forest, the house (designed by Joseph Esherick, for whose home Halprin had created a garden in 1951) features several interior courts and a "garden living room" stepping up to a paved, terraced expanse of basins and water channels. An early example of Halprin's debt to Spanish gardens, the McIntyre design displays his delight in water and all its qualities. The Caygill, McIntyre, and Simon roof gardens, along with the Donnell garden, were

Fig. 7. Simon roof garden, Telegraph Hill, San Francisco, 1952. Courtesy LHC.

included in the Museum of Modern Art's landmark publication *Modern Gardens and the Landscape* (1964), contributing to Halprin's growing reputation and extending the influence of his work.[15]

Of the residential gardens he created during the early 1950s, the one he created for Anna and himself and their two young daughters, Daria (b. 1948) and Rana (b. 1952), held the most personal significance. The Halprin home, designed by William Wurster, was located in Kentfield, Marin County, in a forest of redwood, madrone, and oak on the slope of Mount Tamalpais. The landscape plan encompasses a series of open spaces, including a brick entry court, a gravel terrace, and a deck built around large redwoods. Halprin and Arch Lauterer, an accomplished stage architect and lighting designer, created its signature feature—the "dance deck" (1952–54) on a forested slope below the house (fig. 8).

Fig. 8. Dance deck, Kentfield, 2013. Photograph by author.

Designed as a place for performance, teaching, and personal expression, the deck became a landmark in the history of avant-garde dance. In 1955, Anna founded the San Francisco Dancers' Workshop, which explored movement, the body, and the role of myth and ritual through "collective creativity." Larry watched and drew the group's activities, sometimes designed their costumes and sets, and, in Anna's words, "advised and collaborated on everything."[16] The Halprins shared the desire of the era for public involvement and for a democratization of actions that affected people's lives. In the cultural arena, this desire was expressed by breaking the bounds of the museum, the gallery, and the concert hall; in the political realm, through grassroots activism, anti-elitism, and participatory and advocacy planning. The dance deck, and the social experience that Anna invested it with, influenced Halprin's subsequent efforts to retain the intimacy of a residential landscape in a public arena—a hallmark of his work.

Halprin expanded his practice to include two Berkeley graduates, Don Ray Carter, who joined the firm in 1950, and Satoru Nishita, who arrived the next year. The new designers were settling in when the firm began to explore opportunities arising from California's educational innovation. The state system of higher education responded to California's exploding population by creating a vast, integrated, and tiered system of junior colleges, colleges, and universities. In the Central Valley, Halprin worked with the architect Robert Evans on the long-range master plan of the University of California, Davis, addressing its expansion from a small agricultural college to a major research university and helping to introduce modernist design to a campus with a Beaux-Arts architectural tradition. Halprin's 1952 plan, and in particular the planting design, responded to the hot, arid, flat landscape. A grid that related to the valley's Jeffersonian agricultural grid established the larger framework, and within it curvilinear forms softened academic and residential courtyards and plazas. Extensive plantings lined separate vehicle, bike, and pedestrian pathways. The design incorporated Putah Creek, which runs through the campus, as both a recreational amenity and an arboretum. The following year, Halprin created a master plan for the campus of UC Berkeley. These projects extended over several decades, as many of Halprin's ideas significantly influenced the character of both campuses.

From 1953 to 1958, Halprin collaborated on Greenwood Common, a community housing project in Berkeley conceived and designed by William Wurster. The complex consisted of eight single-family homes clustered around a common area on a two-and-a-half-acre site; design guidelines regulated the homes and established a carefully calibrated relationship between the common area and private gardens (fig. 9).

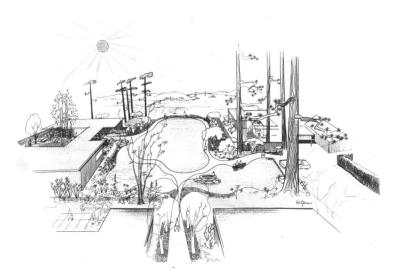

Fig. 9. Greenwood Common, Berkeley, drawing, c. 1950. Courtesy LHC.

Halprin's landscape design focused on the central green, with its Monterey pines and dramatic view of the bay, to which he added a striking plum allée as an entry. He also designed four individual gardens.[17] Years later Halprin would note the influence of his communal experience at the kibbutz and cite Greenwood Common as a precursor to design concepts that he expanded on at Sea Ranch. The housing project quickly became a showcase of Bay Area modernism.

In 1955, Halprin landed a commission that would launch his firm in new directions. His first commercial project, Old Orchard Shopping Center in Skokie, Illinois, was an opportunity for Halprin to make his mark in conjunction with a new building type, the suburban shopping center. His plan extended residential concepts of outdoor life and outdoor rooms to the scale of a commercial complex, creating a "garden for shopping." Richard A. Vignolo, a graduate of Berkeley and the Harvard Graduate School of Design who joined the firm that year, completed the detailing on the Old Orchard drawings.[18] The developer of the project, Philip Klutznick, hired Halprin and the same architectural firm to design the Oakbrook Shopping Center several years later.

Halprin returned to Israel in 1955 to accept his first international commission, the landscape design for the Weizmann Institute of Science in Rehovot. This project established his modus operandi for ongoing work in Israel, a combination of design and consultation in which Israeli practitioners would execute much of the work.[19] Two years later Halprin returned to design the open space for the Hebrew University, Givat Ram campus in West Jerusalem, a plan distinguished by a vast checkerboard-like central plaza at the core of the site (fig. 10). He also became a respected adviser on the development of Israel's national parks and nature reserves.[20]

Fig. 10. Hebrew University, Givat Ram campus, Jerusalem, c. 1960. Courtesy LHC.

Beginning in 1959, Halprin kept "a professional diary or travelling office if you will" in the form of a series of notebooks.[21] Over the course of his life he would fill 127 volumes with diagrams and drawings, ideas for projects, drafts of articles, letters and speeches, spontaneous responses to places, and sketches of people as well as a series of revealing self-portraits. In addition to enriching his work with these personal records, Halprin began to expand his office. He hired Sue Yung Li Ikeda, a Berkeley graduate and designer who would later become a partner in the firm, and Jerry Rubin, who would prove an invaluable office manager.

In 1960, having assembled a talented interdisciplinary team, Halprin incorporated his practice as Lawrence Halprin & Associates. Collaboration was fundamental to Halprin's philosophy, and he continued to expand his professional infrastructure, ultimately hiring artists, social scientists, psychologists, graphic designers, geographers, ecologists, and photographers. His office would collaborate with some of the finest Bay Area architects—William Wurster, Joseph Esherick, Charles Moore, William Turnbull Jr., and Donlyn Lyndon.

Halprin prided himself on his mastery of all stages of the design process—from conception and preliminary drawings to construction documents, building methods, materials, and supervision—but he also relied heavily on the expertise of his staff. Supported by skilled professionals, Halprin's dynamic personality, his ability to communicate, and willingness to take risks quickly propelled his firm to the upper echelon of the profession and established its national reputation for innovation and quality. It was a period of investigative, creative, and imaginative collaboration, and the practice was truly a trailblazing enterprise.

It hardly seems coincidental that Halprin's most dramatic and recognizable innovations were made during this time of intense focus on the creative process. In a series of designs for Portland, Oregon, Seattle, San Francisco, Denver, Fort Worth, and Rochester, New York, he reimagined the possibilities of American civic spaces. His fascination with the role of water in the garden as a central design element was already apparent in residential projects that incorporated the ubiquitous California swimming pool—the Donnell garden in Sonoma and the Schuman garden in Woodside, for example—and in the McIntyre garden's fountains and water channels. These modest gestures were preliminary exercises, as he came to reconceive the urban fountain as a locus of city life.

At Seattle Center Halprin designed the master landscape plan for the World's Fair (1962) and the site's ultimate transformation into a park and cultural center. At the base of the

Space Needle, a grand lagoon contains the Water Sparkler, an innovative fountain that Halprin designed in collaboration with the sculptor Jacques Overhoff. The fountain was inspired by historic water gardens, which derived from the geometry and properties of irrigation systems. The Water Sparkler used the forms and technology of contemporary standard agricultural irrigation equipment in a novel way, creating an ensemble of pipes, valves, and 145 sprinkler heads from which water jets, sprays, and spins.

In the 1960s, numerous American cities were converting their downtown areas into pedestrian malls as a way to revitalize their economies as well as to reinvigorate street life. At the time these projects were seen as progressive, but most of them were ultimately deemed failures, and many of the malls were returned to vehicular use. Halprin's efforts had sporadic success. His redesigns always responded to each street's unique urban situation, whether a thousand feet or three miles long. In all of his designs Halprin applied the insights he had noted in *Cities,* paying close attention to the details of street furniture, benches, drinking fountains, lighting, paving, planting, signage, bollards, and kiosks to establish a choreography of elements that gave primacy to the pedestrian experience. Of the approximately two hundred downtown streets that were converted to pedestrian or transit malls in the United States during this period, fewer than thirty remain as such. Halprin designed two of them.

In 1962 the Halprin office was commissioned to redesign Minneapolis's Nicollet Avenue, a major downtown shopping street (fig. 11). The reconfigured avenue, Nicollet Mall, was not a purely pedestrian thoroughfare, however: its serpentine configuration accommodated buses and so functioned as a transit mall, the first in the nation. In 1976 the firm trans-

Fig. 11. Nicollet Mall, study model, c. 1965. Courtesy LHC.

formed East Main Street in Charlottesville, Virginia, into the Downtown Mall. Designed through a series of community workshops, the mall was paved in brick and punctuated by willow oak "bosques" and street furniture, with lighting commissioned specifically for the site. The project revitalized Charlottesville's historic downtown, and the street is now an entertainment district filled with restaurants, shops, and theaters. Twenty-five years after its completion, when the mall was in need of renovation, an effort by the community and Halprin experts preserved the fundamentals of the original design.

The city was Halprin's primary concern during this time, but he also directed his energies to projects beyond the urban arena. In the early sixties he led the planning effort for Sea Ranch, a landmark collaborative project located one hundred miles north of San Francisco on the wild Northern California coast (1962). The landscape and community design for Sea Ranch went beyond a conventional study of landscape constraints and opportunities by utilizing an ecological analysis to inform planning considerations and design criteria (fig. 12). According to the landscape architect Kathleen John-Alder, "The coastal site allowed Halprin to delve into a deeper and more personal reading of ecology that encompassed community formation, systems thinking, Gestalt theory, art and evolution."[22]

The new firm eagerly took on other groundbreaking commissions, such as the multifamily housing cluster at St. Francis Square in the Western Addition section of San Francisco. This racially integrated cooperative housing complex, sponsored by the International Longshoremen's and Warehousemen's Union, was designed by the architects Robert Marquis and Claude Stoller in 1960. Like many projects of the era, it resulted from an urban renewal initiative that

Fig. 12. Condominium One, Sea Ranch, 2013. Photograph by Carol M. Highsmith. Courtesy Jon B. Lovelace Collection of California Photographs, Carol M. Highsmith Archive, Library of Congress, Prints and Photographs Division (CHA).

demolished all houses in the area, removing residents and offering developers a clean slate. The project was a super-block of 299 three-story units clustered around three common greens and play areas, with parking at the periphery. An existing YMCA and an elementary school were retained and integrated into the overall plan.

The St. Francis Square project marked the first of many commissions in which Lawrence Halprin & Associates found itself at the forefront of innovative and socially conscious environmental design. In a post-occupancy evaluation of the project, Clare Cooper Marcus, a Berkeley environmental psychologist, concluded that the attention given to the site plan and to the landscape design was the key factor in the project's success.[23] The open spaces fostered social interaction and were especially significant as safe places for children, who were the main users. More than fifty years after its completion the complex is still a desirable place to live. Meticulously maintained by the cooperative, the landscape plan includes ornamental gardens in a courtyard, mature plantings, and the later addition of rooftop solar panels. Residents are adamant about fighting any encroachment on the open spaces of the community. Years earlier Halprin had noted that private garden areas were needed in the kibbutz as a counterpoint to the predominant communal areas. At Greenwood Common and at St. Francis, Halprin responded to this earlier realization by providing the necessary balance of private and public space.

From his early years as a designer, Halprin dreamed of creating places for events to happen, but he could hardly have imagined a more ideologically appropriate setting for his work than the Berkeley campus. In 1962, working with the architects Vernon DeMars and Donald Reay, he designed Sproul Plaza and the Student Union grounds off

Fig. 13. Sproul Plaza, University of California at Berkeley, 2008. David Schmitz Photography.

the Telegraph Avenue entrance to the university (fig. 13). Two years later, his design would serve as the stage for the birth of Berkeley's Free Speech Movement—a key event in the development of 1960s radicalism, the antiwar movement, and the emerging counterculture. The plaza fronts Sproul Hall, originally the administration building, whose steps were the site of the demonstration. The classical design features an entry promenade, with an allée of plane trees providing shade and direction, leading to a large brick-paved gathering space. Off to one side is a simple fountain and pool surrounded by a seating wall.[24] In designing Sproul Plaza, Halprin not only encouraged social interaction, as he had hoped, but also became forever associated with a monument to the movement.

Halprin's work for the University of California, Santa Cruz, brought him together with his mentor Thomas Church, who served as the landscape architect for the campus's Long Range Development Plan (1963). Led by the architect John Carl Warnecke, the team created a radical master plan for a university composed of residential colleges based on the British models of Oxford and Cambridge. Unlike their urban counterparts, however, the UC Santa Cruz colleges would be tucked within a redwood forest bordering a vast meadow overlooking Monterey Bay. As the landscape architect for the first three colleges—Cowell, with the firm of Wurster, Bernardi & Emmons; Stevenson, with the architect Joseph Esherick; and Crown, with the architect Ernest J. Kump—Halprin played a significant role in highlighting the dramatic natural beauty of the site (1963–67).

The year he completed Sproul Plaza, Halprin began another project of creating spaces for social interaction, but in this case with the goal of giving new life to an outdated cluster of industrial buildings. The transformation of the

Ghirardelli Chocolate Factory in San Francisco into Ghirardelli Square (1962–68), a popular tourist attraction, became the prototype for scores of similar conversions around the nation, what would become known as the "adaptive reuse" of derelict manufacturing and commercial enterprises. It also inspired the development of "festival marketplaces" as foci of city life. Modeled after European examples, these marketplaces were the early harbingers of a cultural shift that would revitalize American street life, give attention to the design of streets as public places, and introduce the now-commonplace outdoor café into the American landscape. Although these changes cannot be credited solely to Halprin, his work epitomized them.

Halprin's efforts to enliven the city continued with Portland's South Auditorium Renewal Project, for which he designed the Open Space Sequence, a progression of spaces that featured two grand civic fountains—Lovejoy Fountain (1966) and Forecourt Fountain (1970). Inspired by his studies of water in the Sierra Nevada, the fountains were conceived as places for performance where people were permitted, and even invited, to participate in the landscape. These designs were radical reconceptions of the urban fountain in both form and function. Condensing and distilling the landscape, Halprin extracted the essence of mountain streams, creating a kind of abstract miniaturization. The *New York Times* architecture critic Ada Louise Huxtable described the aesthetic as a "geometric naturalism."[25] She also considered Forecourt Fountain "one of the most important urban spaces since the Renaissance," an indicator of the excitement the fountains generated. Lovejoy and Forecourt Fountains contributed to Halprin's burgeoning international reputation and remain pilgrimage sites for tourists and designers alike.

As he contemplated the challenge of the city, Halprin

also took on the issue of freeways—another subject he recognized as a central design problem of our time. In his book *Freeways* (1966), based largely on reports his office had prepared for the California Division of Highways (Caltrans), Halprin lamented, as others had, that road design had become the sole province of engineers. He viewed freeways as potentially great works of contemporary art, extolling the thrill of moving at high speeds. He described the task of designing a highway out in the countryside as one of "landscape politeness" and as "a form of action calligraphy" that entails "an exercise in choreography in the landscape."[26] In the city, the freeway offered a new kind of urban experience and viewpoint, yet Halprin could not deny the destructive impact of the freeway and the automobile on the environment, and especially on communities.

A decade later in Seattle he used the freeway as an urban design element at Freeway Park (1976), where he merged the roadway with a grand fountain. The park featured water in the form of a cascading concrete canyon, but this was not a simple civic plaza. The park was constructed over Interstate 5, which had sliced through the city, cutting one neighborhood off from the next. Freeway Park bridged the freeway and reconnected the residential areas on the city's slope with the downtown. A rare innovative example of "air rights development," which entails building in the unused space above transportation infrastructure, the project was a precedent for other parks built over roadways.

In the mid-1960s, Halprin honored his mother by working on the master plan for the Hadassah Medical Center in Ein Kerem, outside Jerusalem. His design included a large square pool with a single jet of water and a square pink limestone step. Halprin also designed the stepped entry promenade and the Ida Crown Plaza of Jerusalem's modernist Israel Museum (architect, Al Mansfeld), which crowns a hill overlooking the valley of the Monastery of the Cross.[27] In 1967, in recognition of Jerusalem's international and sacred significance, Mayor Teddy Kollek assembled a distinguished group of advisers—international architects, planners, historians, artists, and religious leaders—with whom he could consult regarding the design and plans for the reunited city. The Jerusalem Committee included Nikolaus Pevsner, Max Bill, Buckminster Fuller, Isamu Noguchi, Louis Kahn, Bruno Zevi, Philip Johnson, Lewis Mumford, and Isaiah Berlin. The lone landscape architect in the group, Halprin offered advice that was not always heeded, yet Kollek found him to be "one of the most dedicated, consistent, and outspoken members" of the group and credits Halprin with helping to "formulate a planning policy for Jerusalem that looks at the large open spaces and gardens as the backbone of the city" and with incorporating citizen participation into the planning process, an uncommon practice in Israel.[28]

Halprin exhorted the committee to address "the bowl surrounding the Old City," making "a plea for an architecture which symbolically does not stand up like a clenched fist facing and threatening the landscape of Jerusalem but lies like an open palm embracing it."[29] For Armon Hanatziv, a hill overlooking the Old City, Halprin designed a master plan that would be his lasting contribution to Jerusalem (fig. 14). He proposed a grand arching promenade to link together neighborhoods and provide a belvedere to one of the world's great vistas and one of its most sacred sites. The proposal was realized as the Haas Promenade, designed with Shlomo Aronson, and the Richard and Rhoda Goldman

Fig. 14. Armon Hanatziv, Haas Promenade, drawing, 1979. Courtesy LHC.

Promenade, designed with Bruce Levin.[30] Both Aronson
and Levin had apprenticed in Halprin's office in the 1960s.
The Tayelet, as the promenade is known locally, is adjacent
to the Jerusalem neighborhood where Halprin lived with his
parents as a teenager.

His urban renewal projects, along with the research for
his books *Cities* and *Freeways,* gave him experience in the
detailed design of individual urban spaces as well as the
broader vision of a city planner. He would work from both
perspectives in 1967, when he took on the commission to
redesign San Francisco's Market Street in concert with the
construction of BART (the Bay Area Rapid Transit system).
Halprin's plan gave continuity to the street—a main diago-
nal that cuts a swath through diverse districts—by widening
sidewalks, planting street trees, and using a unified palette
of materials (fig. 15). His work along Market Street included

Fig. 15. Market Street, San Francisco, pen and ink drawing, 1970s. Courtesy LHC.

Hallidie Plaza, an entrance to a BART station, and United Nations Plaza (1975), with a fountain area that was subsequently linked to the city's Civic Center. The street terminated near Embarcadero (Justin Herman) Plaza (1962–72), a vast brick space Garrett Eckbo declared "as handsome a piece of inspired Neo-Renaissance geometry as one can find."[31]

Fig. 16. Embarcadero Fountain, San Francisco, 2013. Photograph by author.

Halprin described Embarcadero Plaza as "a theater for events to happen."[32] As a centerpiece, he outlined the concept of an interactive concrete fountain that offered the possibility of walking behind a waterfall, like the Ovata Fountain at Villa d'Este in Tivoli (fig. 16). Halprin served on the design competition jury that awarded the commission to the French Canadian artist Armand Villancourt. Critics both applauded and derided the fountain, whose powerful flow drowned out the nearby automobile traffic.[33] The plaza was originally bounded on one side by the elevated Embarcadero Freeway, which restricted access to the bay. The edge beneath the freeway had a continuous seating wall warmed by the sun. With tragic irony, the brutal forms of the fountain were likened to California after an earthquake; when the freeway was demolished after the 1989 Loma Prieta earthquake, sections of the plaza were redesigned, and it lost some of its vitality.

Lawrence Halprin & Associates continued its cutting-edge analysis of the urban condition with *New York New York* (1968), a report undertaken on behalf of the New York City

Department of Housing and Urban Development. The study began by focusing on open spaces in urban renewal areas and evolved into an urban open space design primer. Addressing the city at multiple scales—from stoop to sidewalk to street to neighborhood—*New York New York* analyzed six sites and offered schematic proposals for improvement. These included the retrofitting and infilling of properties with ample provision for new open spaces that would address neighborhood identity and local needs. The pioneering urban ecological study also looked at opportunity areas such as rooftops and explored the key open space of the city—the streetscape—while giving due attention to sun, light, wind, precipitation, orientation, and building mass. Policy and zoning recommendations were included. Perhaps Halprin's greatest contribution to modernist landscape architecture was his steadfast belief in the value of America's cities and his plans for saving them.

The firm used *New York New York* as a model for reports on two very different cities, producing the *Hennepin Avenue Report* (1969) for Minneapolis and the *Everett [Washington] Community Plan* (1972). Both projects made use of the bioclimatic approach to architectural regionalism described by Victor Olglay in his classic work *Design with Climate* (1963). Bioclimatic design had rarely been applied at a city scale, and the studies became pioneering experiments in what subsequently became known as urban ecological design. Although the reports largely remained on shelves, they offered an alternative to common zoning practices and are precedents, if often unacknowledged, for the urban designs and plans undertaken in recent years.

The success of Halprin's projects in Portland led to work on an even larger scale—a seminal regional planning project summarized in *The Willamette Valley: Choices for the Future* (1972). The report offered profusely illustrated scenarios for future development of the Willamette Valley, which is home to the bulk of Oregon's population. Like *New York New York,* the Willamette Valley report was conceived as an "environmental primer," and it helped catalyze support for the groundbreaking statewide land use planning law passed the following year under Oregon governor Tom McCall.

Throughout the sixties, Halprin explored the contrast between natural and urban settings, both through the variety of his commissions and in his more personal explorations into the creative process. In 1966, and again in 1968, Larry and Anna hosted a month-long series of joint workshops called "Experiments in Environment" that became a hallmark of their legacy. They staged the events on the dance deck, at Sea Ranch, and in San Francisco—a domestic, a wild, and an urban setting. The participants were dancers, designers, and artists. At Sea Ranch the most notable session centered on the building, destruction, and rebuilding of a "driftwood village" on the beach (figs. 17, 18). It was an ephemeral com-

Fig. 17. Driftwood Village, Sea Ranch, 1968. Courtesy LHC.

munity built with the basic materials of sand and driftwood, materials echoed in Anna's later works in which she explored nature's primal materials of rock, sand, water, trees, and sky. This limited palette was sometimes employed in Larry's subsequent works as well. Photographs of Driftwood Village became counterculture design icons. In 1970 the Halprins' workshop was scored as a month-long City Dance project in San Francisco. Although the counterculture was largely a youth movement, Larry and Anna embraced the tenets with a verve, engaging in its rituals, rites, and changing attitudes toward work, sex, drugs, and convention. Halprin's designs attempted to infuse places with the democratic and participatory ethic of the era.

Under Anna's influence, Halprin's passion for movement morphed into an interest in choreography. In *Cities* he wrote that "the city comes alive through movement and its rhythmic structure," where the urban elements are animated and contribute to "the choreography of the city."[34] The etymology of "choreography" is *choreo,* "dance," and *graphy,* "writing." Like the architects and planners Philip Thiel, Kevin Lynch, and Donald Appleyard, Halprin experimented with notation systems and methods to represent movement graphically—in other words, the choreography of spaces. Halprin coined the term "motation" for his idiosyncratic notation system. This concern with movement, urban choreography, and the use of motation was manifested in many of Halprin's subsequent designs—notably the Nicollet Mall in Minneapolis, the Downtown Mall in Charlottesville, Market Street in San Francisco, and the Haas and Goldman Promenades and Ben Yehuda pedestrian mall in Jerusalem. He recognized that street design contributes more to the quality of urban life than any other factor.

In 1969, Halprin articulated and formalized his design

Fig. 18. Halprin at Sea Ranch reading the score for his workshop, 1968.
Courtesy LHC.

The RSVP Cycles

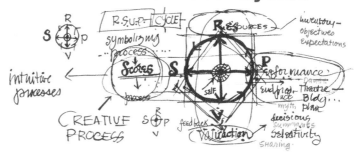

Fig. 19. *The RSVP Cycles: Creative Processes in the Human Environment* (1969), draft of cover design. Courtesy LHC.

method with the publication of *The RSVP Cycles: Creative Processes in the Human Environment* (fig. 19). The letters RSVP, while suggesting responding to an invitation, are an acronym for Resources, Scores, Valuaction, and Performance. In his quest "for means to describe and evoke processes on other than a simply random basis," Halprin appropriated the term "score" from the performing arts world and expanded its meaning to include any representation that determines a "performance," whether one as ephemeral as a dance or one as permanent as a monument. Scores "are *symbolizations of processes* which extend over time," and he saw scores as "a way of describing all such processes in all the arts, of making process visible."[35] Since most processes remain invisible, scores foster communication with others and allow for "participation, feedback, and communications."

As Halprin explored the direct correlation between scores and performances, he realized that he needed to incorporate "resources" and "valuaction" (a term he coined) into the process. Resources include all forms of information related to a project, such as inventories, mapping, questionnaires, legal and financial data, and the concerns of users and clients. Valuaction is the analytical phase that enables evaluation and demands judgment. Halprin diagrammed the four elements of the RSVP process as a circle, with all components interacting, and suggested that the design process can begin at any point along the circle. Although the four components of the RSVP process are presented as equal in importance, the score is the catalyst and performance is the desired result. The attention to the graphic dimension of scoring is not surprising. In the introduction to a collection of writings from the Notebooks published in 1972, Halprin explained, "People 'think' in different ways, & I find that I think most effectively graphically & also that my thinking is influenced a great deal by my ability to get it down where I can look at it & think about it further—the process of thinking with me generates more thinking."[36] The RSVP method evolved to become his methodological signature.[37]

Halprin's drawings (or scores) demonstrate his remarkable ability to capture the essential qualities of a place and succinctly conceptualize landscape design at multiple scales. They reflect how people move through the landscape—where they stop to look and what attracts their attention, as well as the sequences of spaces and the layers of time and space, what the city planner Kevin Lynch called the "temporal collage."[38] His scoring investigations, and the examples he used to explain the concept of scoring, brought together conventional methods, such as orchestra scores and labanotation (a system for recording and analyzing human movement), and experimental divination techniques, such as the I Ching, Tarot, and astrology. The music of John Cage, happenings, and the precursors to performance art also influenced Halprin's theory and practice.

Halprin believed that his RSVP cycle formula had broad

applicability and could function at the personal level as well as with groups or communities. The framework for a variety of performances, a score might result in something as impermanent as a dance, happening, or workshop or as enduring as the construction of a civic space. Scores encouraged improvisation and the unexpected. Halprin surely had expectations of how a place would function, but he also took pleasure in seeing places used in ways that he had not imagined. He emphasized that, when working with others, the designer orchestrates the process, identifies resources, and informs the criteria for evaluation: "By being explicit and by making his struggles and scores visible he accepts responsibility."[39] Although he often proclaimed that the results of a score were not predictable and that he was open to any response, he steered the process in a particular direction based on his values and his desire to encourage participation. As Kathleen John-Alder notes, Halprin "complicated his argument by positioning the designer in the dual role of impartial observer and partial orchestrator."[40] His was also an inherently positive approach, founded on the underlying belief that "scores are not goal-oriented, they are hope-oriented"[41] (fig. 20).

Halprin often ruminated on his role as a designer. In "Thoughts on Design" he rebelled against "a garden in which all is fixed is limited in time and space and humanity." He admired "a garden which is enhanced by chance occurrences which is enriched by weeds and suckering growth and the changing patterns of sunlight and shade and the branch falling on the terrace. It is better because I am part of it. It is not finished."[42] Such thoughts anticipated the significance he would place on performance as the goal of design. As early as 1961 he questioned: "Am I a landscape architect who builds everything architecturally (as Noguchi) and 'artisti-

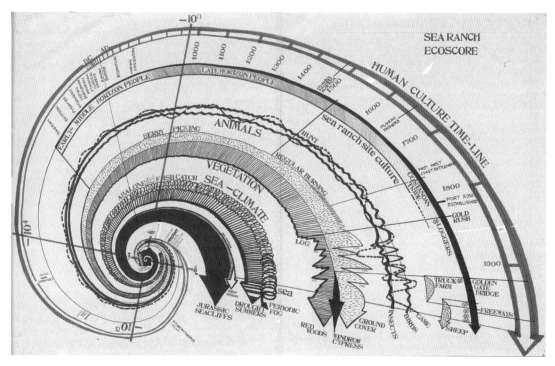

Fig. 20. "Sea Ranch Ecoscore," 1962. Courtesy LHC.

cally' or tried to make everything look natural the fact is and of course I do both. But the point is different. The point is, I believe, less *form* in design as an envelope, which is *placed around things.* What I want is to design *events,* which occur . . . which have no necessary or recognizable *forms* but which generate qualities of experience. . . . Against that I am bored stiff with architecture which has 'form' no matter how beautiful because form is evanescent and intellectual and transient whereas experience in depth of perception is constant."[43]

By 1970, Lawrence Halprin & Associates had expanded to fifty individuals and gained a reputation as a place where progressive landscape architects aspired to work. That year's office brochure included a group photograph, with everyone assembled on the office stairs and balcony. (In a similar, well-known photo that did not appear in the brochure all the participants are nude.) The gathering of Halprin's team for the photo belied problems in the office, however; there was dissatisfaction within the remarkably diverse ensemble of creative individuals. The previous year Halprin had written his partners a long letter outlining the state of the office, which was clearly in a state of stress and transition. In retrospect, it appears that Halprin's effort to create a collaborative environment was not altogether successful. Younger associates were demanding their say in office policy, and there were problems in the administration of the firm. Reflecting the times, and perhaps encouraged by Halprin's own philosophy, the staff objected to the hierarchal organization of founder, principals, associates, and workers. Nevertheless the practice continued to thrive in the early 1970s, building on its reputation for offering innovative solutions to contemporary issues. Asserting the primacy of landscape architecture in design, Halprin undertook innovative projects at every scale: campuses, urban design, transportation planning, housing, community design, historic preservation, and landscape planning.

The introduction to the firm's brochure emphasized its "all-encompassing" approach to design. Although Halprin spoke of addressing the rural landscape, transportation, and new communities, however, his focus was on rehabilitating the American city. "We believe that existing cities are salvageable but require enormous effort to reconstitute. In this they require the participation of the people who live in them and we involve ourselves deeply in interaction with them as well as the physical environment."[44] His office became engaged in the creation of sites—streets, malls, parks, plazas, fountains, roads—that were not only memorable but also catalysts for change. Halprin viewed the city as a biological community subject to natural processes, and the urban workshops he pioneered were vehicles to help direct and facilitate beneficial changes in the fabric of the city.

What began for Halprin as a series of experimental workshops evolved into "Take Part," a codified method of engaging clients that would benefit his effort to revitalize the city. Halprin inaugurated the Take Part process at the city scale in Fort Worth and Everett, Washington, in 1969, and in Charlottesville, and Cleveland in 1973. In each city he initiated the process in response to a desire within the community for environmental change. Take Part attempted not only to elicit ideas from participants but to engage them in the issues that affected their lives. To enhance participants' awareness of their environment, Take Part workshops utilized existing models and developed others, including environmental awareness activities, the construction of environments, and collective decision making. The professional's task was to translate ideas and insights generated in these workshops into physical designs and policy. Paul Baum, a student of Anna Halprin's who had become a psychologist, helped organize many of the events, along with Jim Burns, a former senior editor of *Progressive Architecture*. The Halprins' Take Part workshops and the publication of *Taking Part: A Workshop Approach to Collective Creativity* (1974), coauthored by Halprin and Burns, had a substantial impact on the design profession; many of the techniques explored are now common practice for community projects.[45] Halprin's reputation for innovative public projects and collaboration were surely a factor in his selection as designer of the FDR Memorial, a commission he was awarded in 1974 and would work on for nearly three decades.

Denver's Skyline Park (1972–75), like Halprin's parks in Portland, was a central element in an urban renewal scheme; it was designed to provide a key connection to downtown

Fig. 21. Skyline Park, Denver, aerial photograph of Block 1. Photograph by Gifford Ewing, 2003. Courtesy Library of Congress Prints and Photographs Division, Historic American Landscapes Survey, HALS CO-1-26.

Denver's 16th Street spine (fig. 21).[46] Envisioned as a linear oasis in the high desert landscape, Skyline Park was inspired by the arroyos of the sandstone foothills of the Front Range of the Rocky Mountains, Denver's backdrop. The park extended for three blocks, with a water feature in each block. Translating the local geology into colored concrete, the fountains combined elements of stepped forms, much like those in Lovejoy Plaza, with eroded cubic forms. The fountains in Skyline Park, like all of Halprin's fountains, displayed the diverse qualities of water, and their design invited public participation. The park could also function as a storm water retention basin—now a common design practice, but one that was rarely employed at the time.

Heritage Park Plaza in Fort Worth, Texas (1976), is a simple rectangle divided into a succession of three squares that gently slope down from the fringe of the city's downtown toward a bluff overlooking the Trinity River. The upper section of the plaza is surrounded by a wall with water flowing over it inscribed with the plan of the original fort. Inside the enclosure is the water source and channels that slice though green terraces planted with live oak trees. The final square continues the terraces but is inscribed in space as an elevated walk above the wooded hillside that incorporates that "wild" landscape into the garden. The quintessentially modern design illustrates a classic progression from city to countryside.

Under pressure from his employees to alter his practices, Halprin decided to break with the firm he had incorporated fifteen years earlier. In 1976, Lawrence Halprin & Associates became CHNMB Associates, a firm headed by former partners of Halprin's, including Don Carter, William Hull, Satoru Nishita, and Byron McCulley.[47] Carter and Nishita completed the work on several projects including Fort Worth's Heritage Plaza. CHNMB designed the Portland Transit Mall, continuing to place the Halprin office stamp on that city. With Sue Yung Li Ikeda, Halprin founded a new studio, the Roundhouse (1975–78), and made a film about Salvador Dalí, *Le Pink Grapefruit*. He was also active in offering community workshops. During this period, he began the design of the FDR Memorial, and for almost a quarter century was consumed by what he considered his most significant work. Although the design evolved over those years, the memorial is clearly a product of his thinking in the 1970s. It was his last great water environment.

Halprin maintained a collaborative relationship with his former partner Satoru Nishita, with whom he designed a park in Denver to commemorate the Nazi massacre of Jews at the Babi Yar ravine in Russia. Completed in 1982, Babi Yar Memorial Park echoes the tragic landscape in its design. An open meadow leads to a circular bowl, at the center of which is a small plaque stating that beneath it lies earth from Babi Yar. Through this powerful gesture a visitor to the memorial is imaginatively transported to the distant site.[48]

In 1979, the year he received the Gold Medal for Distinguished Achievement from the American Institute of Architects, Halprin ended his three-year partnership with Ikeda and established the Office of Lawrence Halprin in San Francisco.[49] He assembled a team that included Paul Scardina, Gary Rudd, Steven Koch, and Dee Mullen, who managed the office and Halprin's affairs, but he never hired more than a dozen employees.[50] One of the new office's first projects was the corporate headquarters of Levi Strauss (1978–82), located at the base of Telegraph Hill, a site Halprin knew well. His design united an urban plaza with a pastoral urban park (fig. 22).

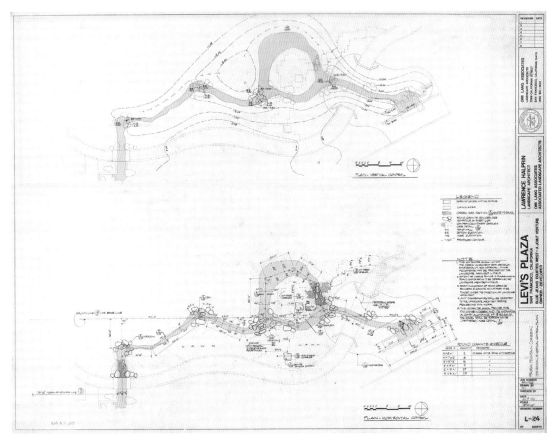

Fig. 22. "Park Fountain (Creek), Levi's Plaza," San Francisco, plan, 1980. Courtesy LHC.

During this period of professional transition, Halprin's mother died. He found solace in designing Rose Luria Halprin's gravestone on the Mount of Olives, visible from the Haas Promenade. At the unveiling of the stone, he spoke of his mother's profound impact on him: "Ultimately it was her value system that influenced me most—she was committed to social betterment—she believed desperately that human beings tho' fallible had the capacity to improve the world and she insisted on devoting her every thought and breath to doing that—not for any reason but that she believed that that is what a human being is all about . . . she gave me that sense of the ultimate morality of being a 'giving' human being and dedicating your life to improving the human condition."[51]

In addition to his ongoing work on the FDR Memorial, Halprin returned to the site of another project he had begun in 1971. Lawrence Halprin & Associates had collaborated with Wurster, Bernardi & Emmons on plans for the Bunker Hill Urban Renewal Project in Los Angeles. Working with Charles Moore, with whom he collaborated on Lovejoy Fountain and Sea Ranch, Halprin proposed a Grand Avenue as the spine of an open space network. The plan was never fully realized, but Halprin designed three of its elements. His Bunker Hill Steps (1983–87), which have much of Moore's postmodern exuberance, were inspired by the Spanish Steps in Rome and terraced Italian water gardens (fig. 23). A hand-level touchable central watercourse parallels a five-

Fig. 23. Bunker Hill Steps, Los Angeles, 2012. Photograph by Carol M. Highsmith. Courtesy CHA.

Fig. 24. Maguire Gardens, Los Angeles, 2013. Photograph by author.

story stairway, whose steps bulge and arc in baroque curves and link to adjacent projects. Like many Halprin designs, the site has become popular with sightseers.

At the bottom of the steps a pedestrian crosswalk leads across Fifth Street to Maguire Gardens (1988), named for the area's developer, Robert Maguire. The garden fronts the Los Angeles Central Library, designed in 1926 by Bertram Goodhue, and presents a dramatic contrast to the steps in character and tone—a place of calm compared with the liveliness of the steps (fig. 24). Halprin respectfully restored and extended elements of Goodhue's axial garden and pools, while adding a fountain court that has both an archaic and a modern feeling reminiscent of the fountain he designed years earlier at the Israel Museum. Several blocks away, adjacent to the Los Angeles campus of the Fashion Institute of Design & Merchandising, is Halprin's Grand Hope Park (1993), a central green space enclosed by vine-covered pergolas and other plantings offering shade throughout the year. For the park's northern corner, Halprin designed a fifty-three-foot-high clock tower adorned with colorful mosaics.

Despite health problems, Halprin remained active into his eighties, and in his later years produced some of his most significant work, all in San Francisco and his beloved Sierra. At Yosemite National Park he redesigned the trail from the lodge to the foot of Lower Yosemite Falls (fig. 25). Much of this design, like that of the Goldman Promenade in Jerusalem, was conceived in the field, on-site, through sketching the design. At another National Park site, a portion of San Francisco's historic Presidio was converted into the Letterman Digital Arts Center, headquarters for George Lucas's film enterprises. The facility's central feature is a seventeen-acre park in which Halprin created the last of his water gardens. Upper-level plazas overlook a stylized stream running through a meadow and ending in a small lake. The plantings and a pergola by the lake frame views of San Francisco Bay and the Golden Gate Bridge.

In a 2003 interview, Halprin described his lifelong inter-

Fig. 25. Lower Yosemite Falls, winter, 2013. Photograph by author.

est in "the use of natural stone, as not only sculpture, but a thematic material to bring back everything to the earth symbolically."[52] His love of stone and water and fascination with their interaction was a continuing theme in his work, one that is present in his drawings of waterfalls and streams in the Sierra. At Sea Ranch he was mesmerized by the ocean waves breaking on the rocky shore. The waves and the seashore can be seen as metaphors for his design methodology—the stone representing the stability of form, a structure in which experience occurs in an almost liquid manner, taking on the shape of the designed container. It seems fitting that Halprin's final commission, completed in 2005, was located in San Francisco and involved creating a place for performance. He transformed Stern Grove, a beloved site of outdoor concerts, into a masterpiece that epitomized his love of working in stone (fig. 26). In this work, and throughout his career, he attempted to emulate nature's performance.

Halprin understood the value and power of communication and engaged the public and his profession with books, articles, exhibits, talks, and appearances. He cultivated a public persona that identified him with landscape and environmental design and was recognized and honored throughout his lifetime, both at home and abroad. During the 1960s, Halprin received a host of professional honors: he was invited to the White House Conference on Natural Beauty in 1965, appointed by President Lyndon Johnson to the first National Council on the Arts in 1966, and selected for the nation's first Advisory Council on Historic Preservation in 1967. He participated in the 1971 International Delphi Conference organized by the Greek architect and town planner Constantine Doxiadis, after which he gained an international reputation

Fig. 26. Terraces at Stern Grove, 2013. Photograph by author.

as a respected adviser. In 1986 the San Francisco Museum of Modern Art featured him in the exhibit *Lawrence Halprin: Changing Places*—a rare honor for a living landscape architect. In 2002 he received the National Medal of Arts awarded by President George W. Bush, seven years before his death October 25, 2009. The posthumous publication of his autobiography, *A Life Spent Changing Places* (2011), is a rare achievement for a landscape architect.

As a mentor and colleague, Halprin extended his influence beyond both his writings and his built work. His San Francisco office provided experience for a remarkable number of successful practitioners including Michael Painter, Richard Haag, Mai Arbegast, Peter Walker, Arye Dvir, Bruce Levin, Nicholas Quennell, Robert La Rocca, Willie Lang, Angela Danadjieva, Simon Nicholson, Dean Abbott, Steven Holl, and Curtis Schreier. Shlomo Aronson, an Israeli architecture student, was inspired to become a landscape architect after hearing Halprin lecture at Berkeley. He went on to work in the San Francisco office before returning to Israel in 1967, where he established his own practice and collaborated with Halprin on the Haas Promenade.

Through the quality of his work and the force of his charismatic personality, Halprin gave his profession a public face. The personal image he liked to cultivate conveyed a certain rugged individualism; he often appeared wearing a cowboy hat, a bolo tie, or Indian jewelry. He helped return landscape architecture to its American origins, defining it as integral to movements for environmental and urban reform, and dispelling elitist associations. According to Laurie Olin, Halprin "helped change how landscape architecture is practiced and . . . understood today."[53] Peter Walker and Melanie

Simo credit him with "redefining the big issues of his time" and describe Halprin as "a towering figure against whom others will inevitably be measured."[54]

Halprin was an innovator in both method and design who created memorable places. His works demonstrate his design skill, attention to choreography and performance, passion for his art, and idealism. While he worked at all scales, he excelled as a site designer, the maker of memorable places. His designs were grounded in a sensitive and imaginative response to the cultural and physical conditions of the site. He had a masterful sense of scale, creating places that are studied calibrations between areas of intimacy and the larger whole. His designs extended the craft, the sense of ownership and identity that individuals feel for their residential landscape, to the public arena. People find comfort within his work, perhaps because he strove for an archetypal quality. Halprin described his art as involving "myths and symbols and basic primitive ideas of what human beings are like."[55] He brought qualities of openness and freedom of expression to his projects, trusting that the places he created would be enlivened by their users—he hoped that people would feel a deep, resonant connection, as he felt in the places that were his touchstones. Anna Halprin put it simply: "Larry wanted people to experience the joy of the landscape."[56]

A significant number of Halprin's landscapes, some of them now several generations old, are canonical works of contemporary design, subject to study, analysis, and preservation. Many others have been remodeled in response to changing fashions, economic shifts, and other factors.[57] When Ghirardelli Square in San Francisco was renovated in the eighties, Halprin bemoaned that it had been "Rousified," a reference to the "festival marketplaces" developed for cities throughout the United States by the Rouse Company, which were partly inspired by Halprin's work. Portions of Ghirardelli Square are now apartments. Heritage Plaza in Fort Worth, so woefully neglected that the city closed it in 2007, was added to the National Register of Historic Places in 2010, a rare recognition for a modern design. The residents of Sea Ranch struggle to assert its original vision. There are significant unbuilt projects—proposals for Jerusalem, Caracas, Milan, Flushing Meadows in New York, the US Virgin Islands—and city workshop ideas that never came to fruition but whose prescient insights are likely to be rediscovered in the future. Manhattan Square Park in Rochester, New York (1971–72), distinguished by a grand space frame over a plaza replete with a skating pavilion, an amphitheater, and a dramatic fountain, was an early success, but minimal maintenance hastened its decline (fig. 27). In recent years the park has been rediscovered and is now used for parkour. People vault over benches, climb and leap across the site's concrete steps and walls, a testament to human imagination and the site's adaptability that would have thrilled Halprin.

Fig. 27. Manhattan Square Park, Rochester, NY, c. 1971. Courtesy LHC.

Fig. 28. Franklin Delano Roosevelt Memorial, Washington, DC, 2006. Photograph by Carol M. Highsmith. Courtesy CHA.

In April 1945, while aboard the USS *Morris,* Halprin and the rest of the crew received the news of President Roosevelt's death. Battle-hardened sailors wept. More than a half century later, in Washington, DC, Larry and Anna Halprin, accompanied by President Bill Clinton and First Lady Hillary Clinton, toured the FDR Memorial following the site's dedication in May 1997. They walked through the four rooms of the memorial, each representing one of Roosevelt's terms and the national response to the Great Depression, World War II, and peace, with sculptures narrating the history (fig. 28). They walked past grand stone walls etched with Roosevelt's inspirational words and past cascading waters and still pools. Franklin Delano Roosevelt is in the national pantheon; so, too, is Halprin, within his chosen profession. He described the FDR Memorial as the "pinnacle" of his career.

"Self portrait before leaving Israel," drawing, April 25, 1998. Courtesy LHC.

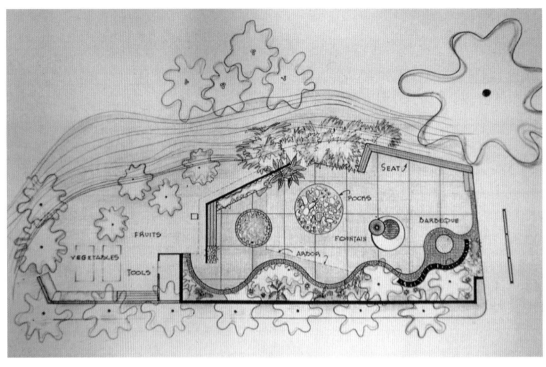

Caygill garden, Orinda, plan, c. 1950. Courtesy LHC.

CAYGILL GARDEN

ORINDA, CALIFORNIA

1950–1951

Halprin's relationship with the Dr. Wayne Caygill and his wife, Theresa, began in 1948, when he took on a commission for the landscape of a house in Moraga Heights, Contra Costa County, while still an associate of the Church firm. His initial design was credited to "Lawrence Halprin—Landscape architect Thomas Church & Associates"; revised plans were solely under Halprin's name. In addition to the contrasting angular and biomorphic forms characteristic of the firm's work, the plan featured a parking court and carport leading to a pathway through a small vegetable and herb garden.

The Caygills hired Halprin to design their second garden, in Orinda, California. It was one of his first projects under his own name and helped him establish an independent professional identity. The garden illustrated one of the central tenets of West Coast residential landscape design: the extension of the home's private realm into the garden.

The concept of the garden room—a hallmark of Thomas Church & Associates and a subject frequently mentioned in popular home and garden magazines—was skillfully manifested here. Halprin's plan and a photograph of his work were the only illustrations for a *House Beautiful* article titled "The Garden of the Next America Is an Outdoor Room." The Caygill garden was also featured in *House and Home* later that year.[1]

When the Caygills hired Halprin to design their second garden, he created an "outdoor room" that broke with the dominant horticultural approach to such commissions. *House Beautiful* described it as "furnished with plants, of course, plus stone, wood, concrete, water, texture, and the deliberately planned play of sunlight and shadow." Individualism and privacy were essential qualities of the garden-as-outdoor-room, in which the designed landscape was exclusively for invited guests. Long, narrow, and roughly rectilinear, with a courtyard-like center, the twenty-five-by-sixty-foot garden was a small but dramatic multilevel geometric composition. As a ground plane, Halprin used a concrete pad scored in a large grid pattern and overlaid with circles and curves. House and garden sat on the flat upper portion of the site, which sloped steeply to a retaining wall and a pool on the north side. A six-and-a-half-foot wood fence screened parking and offered privacy.

In "Notes on the Caygill Garden," Halprin wrote that a "single dominant design feature seemed imperative to hold the divergent elements together." His solution was a sinuous brick wall, which served both as seating and as a planter, with a fence behind it that ran "the length of the garden—curving to widen and narrow the shallow space and thus to make it 'move.'"[2] Opposite the final curve, an angular wooden bench provided additional seating at

View of garden, 1951. Courtesy LHC.

the edge of the slope. A lath structure partially covering the west portion of the garden offered shade and dramatic shadow patterns. The soft curves of the surrounding hills seemed almost part of the private garden.

Within the grid, four perfect circles were placed in a balanced composition, an aesthetic demonstrating the influence of modern artists, particularly the biomorphism of Joan Miró and Jean Arp, whose work had also played a role in the design of the Donnell garden several years earlier.[3] These distinctive forms stood in sharp contrast to the straight lines of fence, bench, lathwork, and grid. Each circle had both a practical and a symbolic purpose. The east circle was a barbeque and fire pit nested within the curves of the stone wall. Nearby, a small pool labeled "wading pool" in Halprin's plans was scaled for a young child, but as the Caygills had no children, offered anyone the opportunity to enjoy the water. This pool was set within a larger concrete circle and fed by a spout to create "audio excitement."[4] The largest, most central circle, eleven feet across, was flush with the patio and contained a composition of stones chosen by Halprin. Shade-tolerant plants were grouped in the final circle, a six-foot-diameter planter beneath the lattice at the opposite end of the garden. Representative of the ancient elements—earth, air, water, and fire—the garden

View with hills in distance, 1951. Courtesy LHC.

design foreshadows Halprin's fascination with Jungian psychology and the power of archetypal forms.

In 1952, Halprin designed a third garden for the Caygills along the famed 17-Mile Drive on California's Monterey Peninsula; his final Caygill garden, for a different home in Orinda, was completed seven years later.

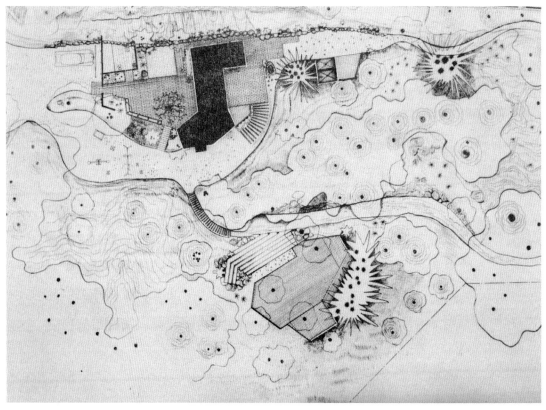

Halprin house and dance deck, Kentfield, plan, c. 1952. Courtesy LHC.

HALPRIN DANCE DECK

KENTFIELD, CALIFORNIA

1952–1954

A long, winding road leads to the Halprin home in Kentfield, Marin County, where Larry and Anna moved in 1952. Larry described the "steep and forested" site as having "immeasurably affected the development of our personal and professional lives."[1] A fenced entrance opens into a brick courtyard that wraps around a three-level house designed by William Wurster. Steps descend to a crushed-gravel court and Anna's office on a lower level, from which additional steps curve back up to a wooden deck adjacent to the dining area and kitchen. Redwood trees ascend through openings in the deck's planked surface.

From the house, another deck is visible between the gnarled trunks and branches of the oaks, madrones, and redwoods covering the steep slope. Although seemingly a conventional California deck, the "dance deck" that Larry and the stage designer Arch Lauterer designed for Anna's performances and classes became a well-known stage in the

Stepped pathway from house, 2013. Photograph by author.

dance world. In 1957, Merce Cunningham performed on it, and the deck quickly became a pilgrimage site for dancers and choreographers.

The downhill path from the house to the deck is a curving procession of railroad tie steps. At the foot of the slope, six rows of backless wooden seats are set among boulders and trees; together with the dance deck, they formed a modest tiered amphitheater. A place to watch rehearsals and performances, the seating area could also become a performance space. The center of the deck is one focus of attention, but the edges—both downstage, facing the seating area, and near the railings, close to the forest—are equally critical. The back of the deck stands thirty feet above the slope and offers a view through the columnar trunks of redwoods. The platform appears to be suspended in the air, the dancers hov-

Dancers on the deck, with San Francisco Bay in background. Courtesy LHC.

Lawrence on the deck with Anna watching, 1966. Courtesy LHC.

ering under the forest canopy. Three madrones originally protruded through the deck, constituting a minimal sort of stage set, but they eventually died and were not replaced. At the rear of the deck and at stage right are small elevated platforms, one of which was initially conceived as an orchestra space. Just beyond stage left is an enclosed conventional dance studio. From the deck, the house can barely be seen through the trees. Both on the deck and inside the home there is a feeling of being enveloped in an arboreal world.

The deck was the site of the Halprins' first joint workshops, which Anna described as "workshopping." She found

Dancers on the deck, drawing, 2002. Courtesy LHC.

"View of Mt. Tam[alpais] from the living room," drawing, March 23, 2006. Courtesy LHC.

Halprin house, drawing, c. 1952. Courtesy LHC.

the spatial structure itself to be "a powerful influence. . . .
The customary points of reference are gone and in place
of a cubic space all confined by right angles with a front,
back, sides and top—a box within which to move—the
space explodes and becomes mobile."[2] The well-worn and
well-oiled surface of the Douglas fir deck is best experienced
barefoot. Dancers respond to small changes in the microclimate, adjusting to areas of sun and shade, light and dark,
and the quiet of the forest. Larry Halprin characterized the
space as "alive and kinetic," and although he didn't dance,

he often watched Anna's rehearsals and performances and constantly drew them. Many of his ideas and methods, particularly those related to the RSVP cycles, motation, and the Take Part process were developed while working on the deck and with Anna.

The intimate experience of creating his Kentfield landscape led Halprin to make design choices that influenced many subsequent projects, including the concrete platforms fronting the cascade at Forecourt Fountain and details at Stern Grove. He described the dance deck as "a world icon of creativity with nature." It also represents over fifty years of personal and professional collaboration. In 2016, Anna and their daughter Daria, as founders of the Tamalpa Institute, were still staging events and offering workshops at Kentfield, known as the Mountain Home Studio.

Old Orchard Shopping Center and parking lots, model, 1956. Courtesy LHC.

OLD ORCHARD
SHOPPING CENTER

SKOKIE, ILLINOIS

1955 (OPENED 1956)

In the mid-1950s the shopping center was a new building type, and with the Old Orchard Shopping Center in Skokie, Illinois, Halprin gave it his stamp. Peter Walker, who was working for Halprin in 1954, recalls that the project began "as a series of small gardens, not unlike the backyards that the office had been building, but the spirit soon grew into something more social and collective, in short, urban."[1] Halprin's solution was to create a network of "shopping gardens" as part of a strolling experience to facilitate movement through the different retail areas. Despite the scale of the endeavor, critics and visitors praised its intimate landscape of bridges, pools, and gardens.

Designed by the architect Richard M. Bennett of the firm Loebl, Schlossman & Bennett, Old Orchard was sited on eighty-five acres about seventeen miles outside of Chicago and consisted of five clusters of buildings, with over sixty shops, arranged around a central Marshall Fields department store. Visitors parked in one of six thousand parking spaces encircling the complex and entered at points behind the buildings into what appeared a vibrant pedestrian "street" of colorful shopfronts. Covered arcades linked the buildings, and open spaces surrounded and connected the stores. Halprin carefully analyzed the site and program, paying particular attention to the movement of shoppers at different times of day and evening. His first design sketches, in 1955, emphasized the pedestrian's constantly changing viewpoint as he or she moved through the landscape. Halprin drew the shopping center as it might appear in each season, in the sun and in the snow.

The client, the Chicago developer Philip Klutznick, of American Community Builders, described the young landscape architect as "afire with ideas" and eager for "the chance to translate his concepts into practice."[2] Klutznick noted that Halprin grossly underpriced his fee, something the landscape architect also mentioned in his autobiography. Not only did Klutznick decide to compensate him fairly, but he also hired Halprin and the architects to design a second complex—the Oakbrook Shopping Center in Oak Brook, Illinois, west of Chicago.

Old Orchard's most dramatic feature was a large area to the north, which comprised a sinuous pool surrounded by rich plantings. Bridges spanning the pool invited shoppers to explore the garden, which featured carefully chosen regional plants to provide interest throughout the year. The primary circulation areas, of pebbled concrete with bricks accentuating the grid pattern, were accompanied by smaller courtyards paved in flagstone like residential patios. Throughout the shopping center, and especially in the courtyards, seating was provided by low stone walls surrounding planted islands. In 1956, the year of the grand opening, the architect Jerrold

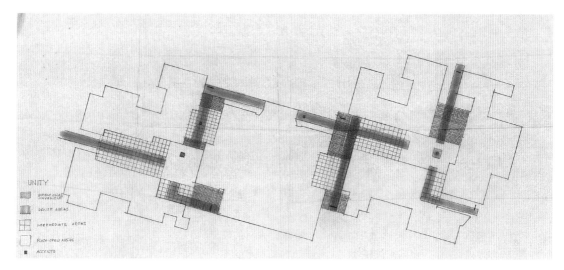

Outdoor circulation patterns, drawing on tracing paper, 1956. Courtesy LHC.

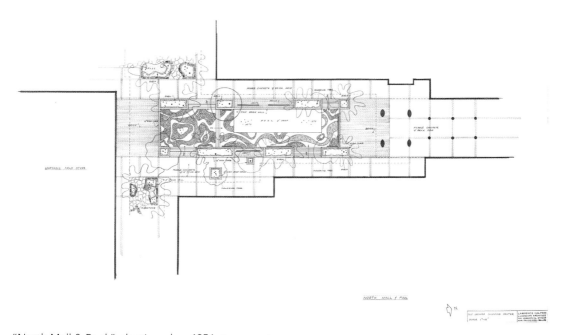

"North Mall & Pool," planting plan, 1956. Courtesy LHC.

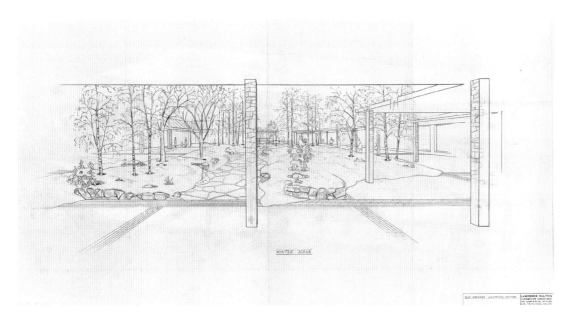

"Winter Scene," architectural rendering, 1956. Courtesy LHC.

"Night Scene," architectural rendering, 1956. Courtesy LHC.

Loebl wrote to Halprin that "everyone, including myself, thinks that the landscaping is quite outstanding and creating quite a stir in the community."[3]

The September 1957 issue of *Architectural Record* included a "Building Types Study" featuring the "large" Roosevelt Field Shopping Center on Long Island, by I. M. Pei, with Robert Zion as the landscape architect; a "small" center in Canada; and Old Orchard as the "medium-sized" example. The article described Old Orchard as possessing "a personality peculiarly its own—one which is both charming and unusual. As one strolls about he becomes pleasantly aware of a scene that changes refreshingly—he finds change of pace, of scale, of direction, of shape, of surface. Yet underlying all is the basic necessity to wholeness. . . . Here is clever planning for business and a delightful environment for humans."[4]

Old Orchard introduced an innovative vision of the modern shopping center experience by providing a location for social gatherings unrelated to its retail purpose. The shopping center's outdoor public areas became locations for concerts and car and flower shows, increasing its popularity as a destination. In the *Architectural Record* article titled "Shopping Can Be a Pleasure," the architect James S. Hornbeck noted that "Marshall Field's is pleased indeed that many people come to Old Orchard on Sundays—when all the stores are closed—simply because it is a pleasant place to be. This is good business."[5]

The architect Victor Gruen included Old Orchard in his book *Shopping Towns USA* (1960), in which he highlights the landscape design and skillful handling of parking areas. Unfortunately, as have virtually all shopping centers of its vintage, Old Orchard has been remodeled and expanded several times, most notably in 1995 by Loebl, Schlossman & Hackl, the successor firm of the original architects. Hal-

Girl playing in fountain, c. 1957. Courtesy LHC.

prin later bemoaned his shopping center experience as representative of rampant suburbanization. However, while few aspects of Halprin's original design survive, Old Orchard remains an open-air mall and the landscape design is still touted as its unique feature.

Main (north) garden area, 1956. Courtesy LHC.

The preserved coastal landscape, Sea Ranch, 2016. Photograph by Chris Thompson.

SEA RANCH

SONOMA COUNTY, CALIFORNIA

1962

In the early 1960s, the architect Al Boeke, vice president of Oceanic Properties, flew over the Northern California coast in search of a location for a new town and spied an expansive ten-mile stretch of windswept coastline 120 miles north of San Francisco. This sublime landscape would become the site for Sea Ranch. The property, only a mile deep, began at the Pacific shoreline, a dramatic confrontation of waves, rocks, small beaches, and coves, with a view extending to the horizon. Above the cliffs lay a grazed terraced meadow punctuated by hedgerows of mature Monterey cypress. The Pacific Coast Highway ran through the meadows, and as the land rose it changed to dense forest of pine, fir, and redwood. Halprin became the master planner for a pioneering project in ecological design that has impacted environmental planning around the world.

This site became Sea Ranch—the translation of Rancho del Mar, the name of the area. The sea was the site's most dramatic natural feature; "ranch" signified its rich history as a cultural landscape. This ranch would no longer serve as productive rural land in a conventional sense, however. It would be transformed into an exurban second-home community, where residents could live in a close relationship with nature.

Halprin was the guiding force on the project, which was distinguished by a collaboration among many disciplines. In planning Sea Ranch, Halprin employed a full range of analytical techniques spanning the most intuitive to the rigorously scientific. He began by immersing himself in the place, walking the entire ten-mile stretch of seashore along the five-thousand-acre site and camping on the property. His dozens of drawings ranged from detailed renderings of rocks and plants to sketches exploring the entire expanse of the ranch. Halprin's analysis is encapsulated in what he called an "ecoscore" diagram, a logarithmic spiral timeline that graphically represents the interaction of geology, sea, climate, vegetation, wildlife, and human intervention. A

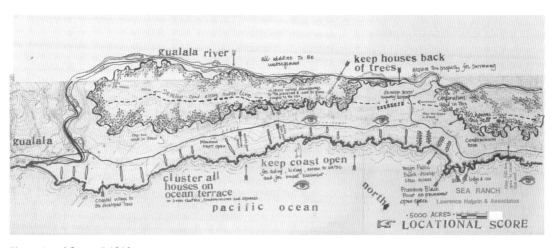

"Locational Score," 1962. Courtesy LHC.

cross section of the spiral is a moment in time; the linear spiral takes the long view. As Halprin has explained, "The value of ecoscores is that they make visible the consequences of action."[1]

A detailed bioclimatic analysis by the cultural geographer Richard Reynolds was a foundation for much of the proposal. The Halprin associate Don Carter used the data on microclimate, especially the effects of wind, to develop a series of grading and planting studies showing how a human comfort zone could be established in this windy, foggy, and rainy coastal landscape. From the analysis propositions were formed on to how to treat the Sea Ranch landscape and ultimately to design proposals. The goal was to protect the essential character of the landscape while allowing those who would be living in the new community to appreciate this unique place. The ranch felt "wild," but it was a domesticated landscape, the product of human activity. The meadows were pastureland for cattle and, most recently, sheep. The hillsides had all been logged. Halprin was inspired by traditional communities and landscapes that had grown organically over centuries, including the indigenous Pomo Indian culture. The challenge was to recreate a quality, a place, and a community with a common concern for this distinctive landscape. Adopting the Pomo philosophy "live lightly on the land," Halprin said his goal was "to inhabit this land and protect the awesome character without softening or altering it."[2] It was an ambitious, even utopian, aspiration—a kibbutznik's desire.

The final proposal identified and addressed Sea Ranch's zones in a cross section. Nothing was to be built directly on the bluffs along the seashore, access points were provided, and views to the sea were to be unobstructed. On the marine terrace, the remnant of an ancient shoreline, buildings were

Path through the common meadows, 2016. Photograph by Chris Thompson.

to be either clustered or embedded against existing hedge-rows. This preserved the meadows as great outdoor rooms, with half the property set aside as common land. The Pacific Coast Highway remained a scenic road with perpendicular access roads running parallel to the hedgerows. Roads conformed to the contours and were constructed without curbs, sidewalks, or storm drains. Houses in the forest were kept back from the meadow edge, and the forest was thinned and managed through selective cutting and controlled burns. No houses were built on the ridgeline. There was no street lighting, thus the sky was given equal status with the earth and the sea.

An ecological approach, coupled with a creative response to the site, led to the development of a distinctive aesthetic in the design of structures, planting, and circulation that

Bluff and meadows, with Lodge in background, 2016. Photograph by Chris Thompson.

reflected the force of the wind, solar orientation, and views. The buildings were designed to blend into the landscape with sloped roofs, and along with windscreens of plantings, fences, and mounding, created outdoor spaces shielded from the wind with maximum exposure to the sun. In deference to the regional character, wood and shingles were the mandated exterior material, building height was limited, and cars were screened and their numbers limited. Indigenous plant material was preferred, and owners were discouraged from "excessive plantings which detract from the natural surroundings"; no lawns or other markers of suburbia were permitted. A program of meadow and hedgerow restoration

Sea Ranch Lodge, 2013. Photograph by Carol M. Highsmith. Courtesy CHA.

Path along the cliff face, 2016. Photograph by Chris Thompson.

was implemented. Ultimately a site design and architectural guidelines were encoded into the Sea Ranch Association's Covenants Codes and Restrictions, and a design review committee was established to approve all new construction and modifications.

Since its inception, Sea Ranch has become an architectural showcase, featuring the work of Charles Moore, William Turnbull, Donlyn Lyndon, and Richard Whitaker, all Berkeley architecture professors. They designed the iconic

Halprin's studio, 2013. Photograph by author.

Condominium One, while Joseph Esherick designed the first cluster of Hedgerow houses. These designers were all immersed in a regional Bay Area design aesthetic and sympathetic to Halprin's plan. As Donlyn Lyndon explained, "We looked to the landscape as mentor, learning from its forces what an architecture of place could become."[3]

Halprin had a cabin and a studio at Sea Ranch for much of his life, and Lyndon, Moore, Turnbull, Whitaker, and Boeke would all build at Sea Ranch as well. The original Halprin cabin designed by Halprin, Moore, and Turnbull had developed incrementally, but was destroyed in a fire in 2001. The outlying separate studio remained unharmed. Halprin rebuilt on the same site with the architects Moore Ruble Yudell and lived there for period of time until his death in 2009. Boeke said the site Halprin chose was the

"Looking down into the cove," drawing, August 26, 2000. Courtesy LHC.

most beautiful at Sea Ranch. Although the guidelines suggested not building on the bluff, Halprin's cabin is not only on the cliff but partly cantilevers over it. The view through the pines is to the variegated seashore and rock outcrops that Halprin drew so often. Walking along the narrow oceanside balcony feels like being on the deck of a ship at sea. There are windows everywhere, looking out from all the rooms.

A small amphitheater is built into the hillside. Constructed largely of driftwood, it surrounds a fire pit and a nearby outdoor kitchen and eating area. Located slightly up the slope, Halprin's studio is marked now by a pylon of abalone shells that previously framed the studio entrance. A 1980

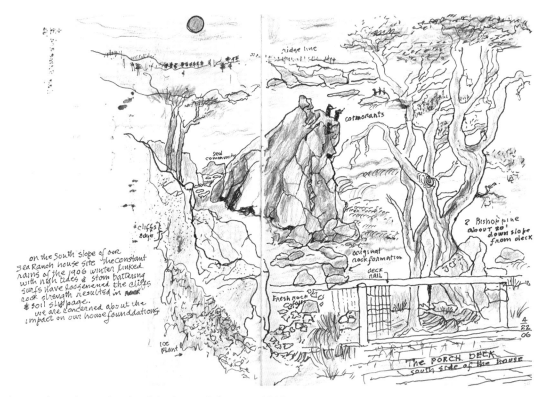

"The Porch Deck, south side of the house," drawing, 2006. Courtesy LHC.

Rebuilt Halprin cabin, 2013. Photograph by author.

Notebook drawing illustrates what he called the "Myths—Symbols—Rituals" that had developed on the site and were "based on family uses, ecological processes and the many varied workshops & people who have participated."[4] Sea Ranch was the site of Halprin's first experimental workshops, offered in 1983, 1993, and 2003 to Sea Ranch residents to revive the original concepts on which the community was based, which he published in *Sea Ranch . . . Diary of an Idea* shortly thereafter. As Kathleen John-Alder has written, the driftwood exercises that took place there were "a proto-ecological, systems based, gestalt field experiment, with the Sea Ranch serving as the spatial laboratory."[5]

Sea Ranch became perhaps the best-known built example of a project that answered Ian McHarg's exhortation to

Ocean view from cabin, 2013. Photograph by author.

"design with nature." In 2014–15, the community celebrated its fiftieth birthday. Over the half century, plantings have matured, vegetation has volunteered, buildings have become bigger and are more scattered, and the generation of pioneers is largely gone. Although much is retained, Halprin was not uncritical of how subsequent development failed to follow the original guidelines as economic concerns superseded ecological stewardship. Controversies with the state over coastal land use and a shift in ownership led to what has been characterized as two Sea Ranches—a southern section, the area first developed, which largely conforms to the original concepts, and a northern section that has been subdivided and has houses along the shoreline and extending out from the forest. Halprin bemoaned the changes that compromised the original vision and disturbed the sense of being in a wild coastal environment. Despite his dissatisfaction, however, he was steadfast in his dedication to Sea Ranch throughout his life. A recently formed Commons Landscape Committee is addressing plans for how its "neighborhoods," as discrete areas are now conceived, can reassert what is characterized as the "Sea Ranch Vision." Sea Ranch offers a method and a model that is too rarely being followed, where thoughtful analysis coupled with creativity integrates the best of scientific and cultural understanding in the making of places.

From his Sea Ranch cabin, Halprin could experience nature's forces at their most powerful and primordial. The energy of the ocean as it confronts the land, the rocks and bluffs of the shore as it rises from the continental shelf, trees clinging to the cliffs and claiming their space in the soil, an endless horizon, and above it all the ever-changing sky.

Nicollet Mall at night, c. 1967. Courtesy LHC.

NICOLLET MALL

MINNEAPOLIS, MINNESOTA

1962/1967

The 1960s have been described as the era of the "malling of America," because of the explosive growth of suburban shopping centers as well as the simultaneous redesign of hundreds of conventional downtown city streets into pedestrian malls.[1] A new relationships between center cities and their periphery was developing as downtowns were losing business to a suburban exodus and the urban core was no longer the focus of public life. The Halprin office was engaged with all aspects of this transformation, commissioned to design shopping centers, adaptive reuses of historic buildings, and revitalizations of city centers.

Minneapolis was at the forefront, with the 1955 opening of the Southdale Mall in suburban Edina, the nation's first enclosed shopping center, designed by Victor Gruen. Various strategies were proposed to counter this phenomenon and help downtowns retain their role as centers of commercial and civic life. The most common strategy was to convert the primary commercial street into a pedestrian mall, removing all vehicles and creating a purely walkable environment (with access for emergency vehicles.) The prototype for pedestrian malls came from Europe, where many cities successfully transformed portions of their historic cores into pedestrian streets after the destruction of World War II. The most notable example was Rotterdam's Lijnbaan (1953), illustrated in *Cities*. Because European cities had high population densities and were designed before the automobile, they thrived with a return to pedestrian use. The conditions in Minneapolis, like most American cities, were different, as was the fate of the newly designed pedestrian zones.

The center city mall design formula was the alteration of the entire street—facade to facade—into a sidewalk, creating a boulevard-like experience interspersed with amenities

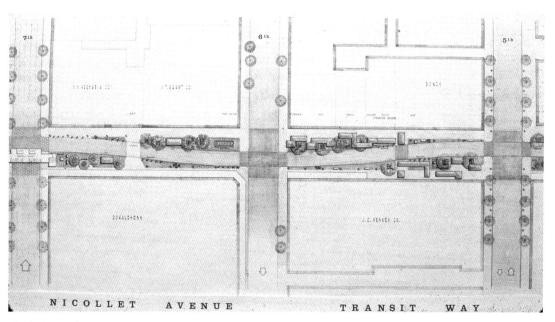

Block detail, drawing, c. 1967. Courtesy LHC.

such as planting, play areas, fountains, seating, and sculpture. One such solution was proposed by Gruen for Fort Worth in 1955; another was executed in Fresno's Fulton Mall, designed by Garrett Eckbo in 1964 as part of Gruen's urban design scheme. In Minneapolis, Hennepin and Nicollet Avenues were the city's commercial heart, a "main street" long past its prime. The Chicago planners Barton-Aschman investigated design alternatives, and in 1961 downtown merchants endorsed their proposal for a curving transit way.

Halprin's design response had much in common with other pedestrian malls, but several factors made Nicollet Mall unique. Most important, it was not purely pedestrian, but was designed as the nation's first transit mall. A twenty-four-foot vehicular right of way was retained, accommodating free Metro buses, taxis, and service vehicles, but no cars. The remainder of the street was given to walkers. The holistic design coordinated all elements from the ground up. The surface was a carefully composed with rhythmic patterns that delineated bus and taxi lanes and pedestrian areas. Over much of its twelve blocks, the roadbed was laid out as a serpentine strand. This configuration created concave and convex areas in the adjacent sidewalk that varied in width from twelve to forty-five feet. In these spaces, in relation with the adjacent shops and traffic flow, Halprin designed a panoply of the urban streetscape elements he had cataloged in *Cities:* site-specific designs for lighting, bollards, benches, street signs, traffic signals, drains, and planters. Featured elements, including a clock tower and fountains, were located in the arcs outlined by the roadbed. Equal attention was paid to craftsmanship and to crafting an experience.

Given Minneapolis's extreme climate, special consideration was given to the winter season. Lighting was designed for the long nights, textured terrazzo pavement and radi-

Block 10, drawing, c. 1967. Courtesy LHC.

Nicollet Mall, c. 1967. Courtesy LHC.

ant heat were installed to melt snow, and bus shelters were
heated. The city's most dramatic response to the weather
was a distinctive elevated climate-controlled Skyway system, begun in 1962 and now eight miles long. However, the
unintended consequence of the Skyway's success was that it

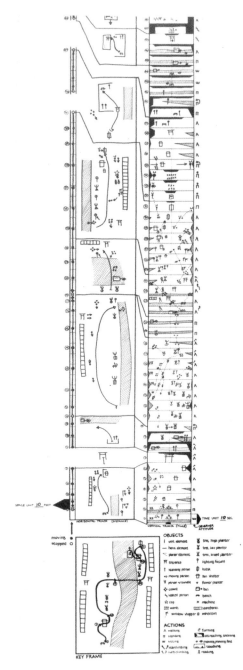

Motation score, drawing by Curtis Scheier, c. 1967.

Courtesy LHC.

removed life from the street level, thus competing with the mall that it intersects.

The Nicollet design was Halprin's most comprehensive use of motation, a graphic notation system for describing movement. His system subdivided any sequence into a series of frames with parallel horizontal and vertical tracks marked with symbols. In applying the system for Nicollet Mall, he subdivided the street into discrete segments. The horizontal track described the movement of people through space as a series of actions: standing, sitting, and turning in different directions. The vertical track highlighted objects: entrances, benches, planters, and lighting, as well

Bus stop, drawing, c. 1967. Courtesy LHC.

as anticipated actions such as window shopping. Further notations offered a suggestion of the speed of pedestrians. In its graphic character, motation approximates the system of musical composition: a score in which the depiction of objects, actions, and locations are equivalent to the notations in sheet music. Halprin's motation clearly expressed his desire to see the street as a coherent composition complete with discrete "movements" and themes with different "instruments" highlighted along the way. The ambitious score could be understood as a tool both for design and for retrospective evaluation. It is difficult to assess whether the motation system accurately predicted how the mall was

Street view, 1967. Courtesy LHC.

experienced, but for many years the project was deemed a success, both economically and socially.

The transit mall eased downtown traffic problems, and Nicollet Mall thrived until the 1980s, when it began a slow downhill slide. Sections had deteriorated, maintenance had been deferred, the snow-melt system failed, and vacancies rose. Despite these issues, the city did not abandon the project. There were proposals to cover some sections in emulation of enclosed shopping centers, which were thwarted. The mall was redesigned in 1990 by the Minneapolis firm BRW, Inc. However, in 1992, the Mall of America opened, increasing competition. Fortunately, Nicollet is in the center of a busy urban district, with 160,000 workers within two blocks and 30,000 residents within walking distance. In 2013 the city, together with the Minneapolis Downtown Council, chose a conceptual design proposal by James Corner Field Operations of New York for a revitalized Nicollet Mall. In many ways a radical revision, it nonetheless retains certain elements of Halprin's design—most important, continuing in the spirit of Halprin's original design to create a festive and inviting atmosphere, an environment of interest and excitement, updated by the fashions of a half century later.

Nicollet Mall was successful in catalyzing additional development in the area and subsuming existing structures into its identity. The mall received national recognition and became the prototype and inspiration for other transit malls, including Denver's 16th Street Mall (designed by Pei, Cobb & Freed, Laurie Olin, landscape architect, in 1982) and Portland, Oregon's twenty-two-block downtown transit mall, designed in 1977 by the Halprin office and its successor, CHNMB.

Ghirardelli Square from San Francisco Bay, 2012. Photograph by Carol M. Highsmith. Courtesy CHA.

GHIRARDELLI SQUARE

SAN FRANCISCO

1962–1968

A huge sign facing San Francisco Bay announces Ghirardelli Square to travelers into the city. Envisioned to be a "beehive of excitement," the complex of five levels of shops, restaurants, and interconnected plazas contains outdoor life in a place that is urbane and animated, civic and commercial, and framed by an innovative urban design. Halprin declared it to be "in a sense a prototype of what the city could be like," demonstrating the impact of his travels on his work.

The Ghirardelli Chocolate Company was founded in San Francisco in 1852 by the Italian immigrant Domingo Ghirardelli. In 1895 he moved his operation to the Pioneer Woolen Mill site overlooking the bay, a site it would occupy for almost seventy years. Like other American ports, the San Francisco waterfront underwent dramatic change in the 1950s. Derelict piers, warehouses, factories, and canneries were demolished. The Ghirardelli complex was up for sale and threatened with a demolition. An enlightened civic leader, the daring developer William Roth, heir to the Matson Shipping Line and the leader of the San Francisco Planning and Renewal Association, purchased the property in 1962. Roth hired Halprin and Wurster, Bernardi & Emmons to imagine how the property might be preserved. Two years later Ghirardelli Square opened, the first large-scale adaptive reuse project in the United States and a landmark in both historic preservation and urban design.

Ghirardelli Square was a resounding economic and social success. It was the prototype for scores of rehabilitations, preservation projects, and "festival marketplaces," a term coined by James Rouse and Benjamin Thompson, the developer and architect of Boston's Faneuil Hall Marketplace and Baltimore's Harborplace. In an article on the "Rouse-ification of Lower Manhattan" the critic Jane Holtz Kay later bemoaned what she called the "Ghirardelli Square syndrome," critiquing the similarity of many projects in adaptive reuse.[1] Communities across the country, however, desired their own Ghirardelli Square. The impact was international. Covent Garden's transformation was described as a "Ghirardelli Square for London."[2]

At the time, the concept was a bold experiment. The red brick exterior shell of the buildings was preserved along with portions of the interior fabric, while the interior machinery and furnishings were gutted. In what became conventional adaptive reuse practice, the image of the site was retained, while the interior was subject to dramatic modification to suit new uses. In a sense, the design mediates between signifying past use and historical association through the exterior and interior contemporary use. The most dramatic features were the retention of the 1915 French Gothic Clock Tower and the reorientation of the huge 25-by-125-foot Ghirardelli sign on a scaffold atop the building to face the bay.

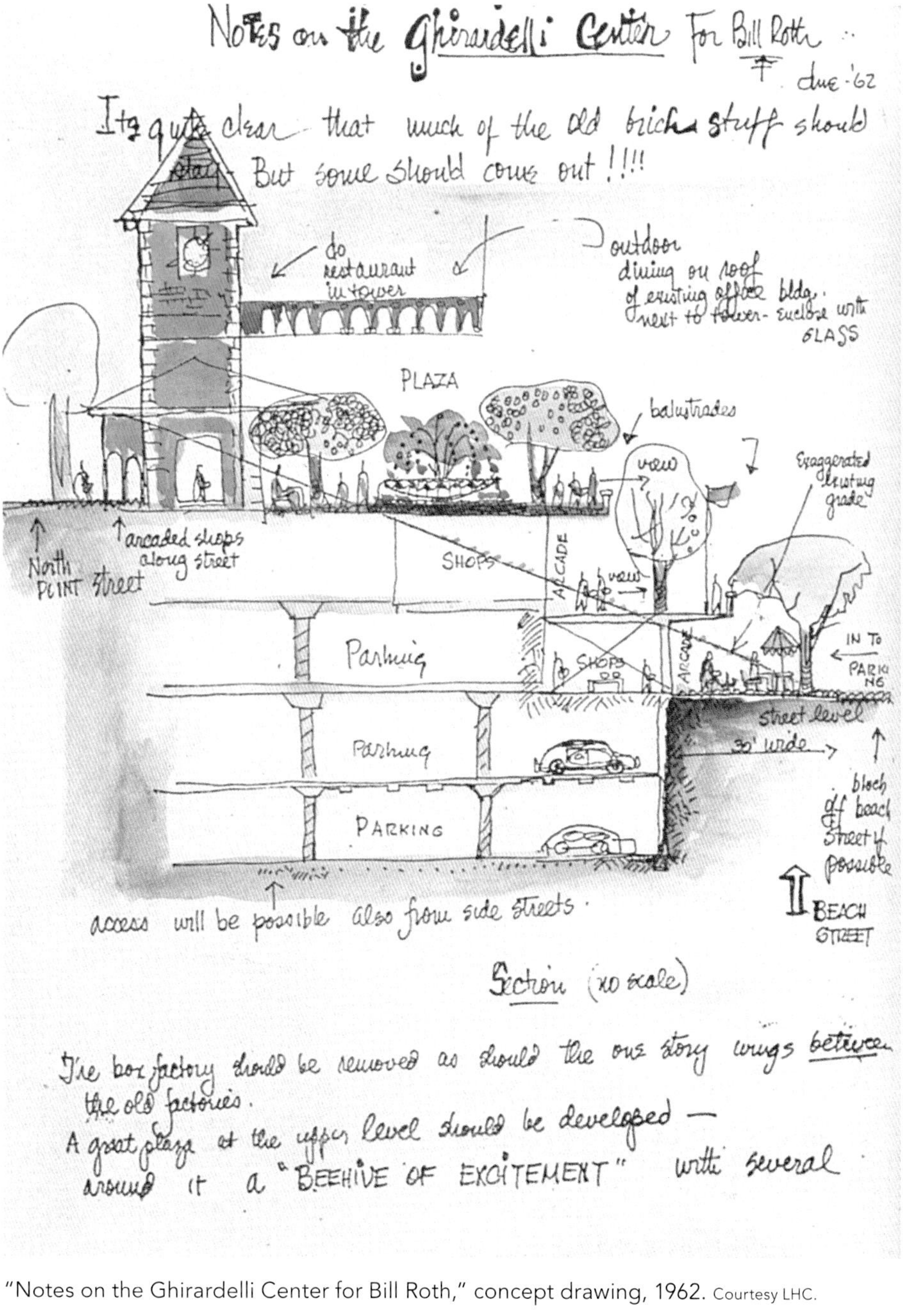
Notes on the Ghirardelli Center For Bill Roth
It's quite clear that much of the old brick stuff should stay. But some should come out!!!!
do restaurant in tower
outdoor dining on roof of existing office bldg. next to tower - enclose with GLASS
PLAZA
balustrades
view
Exaggerated existing grade
arcaded shops along street
North POINT street
SHOPS
ARCADE
view
Parking
SHOPS
ARCADE
IN TO PARKING
street level
30' wide
block off beach street if possible
Parking
PARKING
access will be possible also from side streets.
BEACH STREET
Section (no scale)
The box factory should be removed as should the one story wings between the old factories.
A great plaza at the upper level should be developed —
around it a "BEEHIVE OF EXCITEMENT" with several

"Notes on the Ghirardelli Center for Bill Roth," concept drawing, 1962. Courtesy LHC.

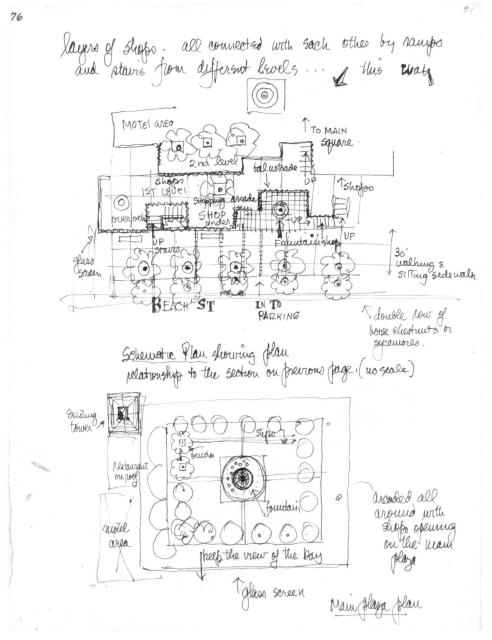

layers of shops - all connected with each other by ramps and stairs from different levels ... ← this way

MOTEL area

↑ TO MAIN square

2nd level

shops 1st level

balustrade

UP

↑ shops

overlook

shopping arcade

SHOP under

↑ UP

UP stairs

Fountain shop

UP

glass screen

30' walking & sitting sidewalk

BEACH ST

IN TO PARKING

← double row of horse chestnuts or sycamores.

Schematic Plan showing plan relationship to the section on previous page. (no scale)

Existing tower

steps

benches

restaurant on roof

fountain

arcaded all around with shops opening on the main plaza

motel area

keep the view of the bay

↑ glass screen

Main plaza plan

"Layers of shops," schematic plan, 1962. Courtesy LHC.

Halprin and Wurster were not timid as they carefully edited the site. The main historic structures—the Chocolate, Cocoa, and Mustard Buildings—were retained. The Box Building on Beach Street was demolished and replaced by the Wurster Building, an arcaded structure facing Aquatic Park at the lower level and bordering the main east courtyard, Fountain Court, on its upper level. In lieu of one large courtyard they subdivided the "square" into east and west sections with smaller one-story shops and playful kiosks. Many critics commented on the debt to Copenhagen's Tivoli Gardens, a Halprin favorite—with both praise and criticism. The west plaza was defined by the sharp angles of the Woolen Mill Building and connected as well to the cascading smaller Lower Plaza and Rose Court. To the east, the largest open area, with a seating capacity of eight hundred for events, had a fountain as its focal point. In early schemes the fountain was a raised basin, but it evolved into a circular pool with seating steps and became the subject of a surprising controversy. The artist Ruth Asawa was commissioned to create a sculpture for the pool. Halprin expected a characteristic abstract work, but Asawa created a figurative ensemble of two mermaids, frogs, and sea turtles. Halprin publicly blasted the sculpture as antithetical to the aesthetic of the square, and the conflict degenerated. The public sided with Asawa, and the mermaids in the fountain prevail as the focal point of the square.

The multilevel site offered dramatic views of the bay, as well as ample opportunities to watch the outdoor activity from tiered balconies. A complex design of ramps and exterior stairs provided access from multiple points, allowing visitors the pleasure of exploring the project. (At the time there were new standards for barrier-free design, but the Americans with Disabilities Act did not become law until 1990). It was a purely pedestrian place. All of the site features and furnishings, the urban elements Halprin cataloged in *Cities,* were individually designed—lighting, seating, planters, railings, trash cans, kiosks, and graphics. A lighted arched entry gateway was built on the Larkin Street side.

In the span of a less than a decade Halprin had designed two innovative suburban shopping centers, at Old Orchard and Oakbrook, and was now engaged with a new kind of retail development. Both project types set the stage for commercial development over the next half century. Both played on a nostalgic appeal to the past. The suburban shopping mall emulated a traditional Main Street, albeit in a much sanitized and often indoor fashion. Adaptive reuse also pulled on nostalgia, but countered by the explicit attempt to introduce urban vitality. Both are also exclusively pedestrian zones. In the shopping center cars are stored at the periphery and at Ghirardelli Square in a four-level underground parking structure. Ghirardelli's tenants followed what became a standard pattern of a mixed blend of smaller specialty shops, restaurants appealing to an upscale and tourist market, and leisure retailing, where shopping is a form of recreation, while shopping centers catered to national chains.

Regardless of the commercial temptations, Ghirardelli Square is an attraction, a place to browse, linger, and just to watch the "action." It became, and remains, a must-see San Francisco site. Entertainment is both programmed and impromptu, with music and street performers in addition to the constant human activity. Significantly, in 1965, Benjamin Thompson & Associates renovated the Clock Tower to house a Design Research store, then the recognized standard bearer of modern design. The success of Ghirardelli Square also catalyzed more immediate local development and preservation. The nearby Del Monte cannery site, once the world's largest, was also threatened with demolition, but was

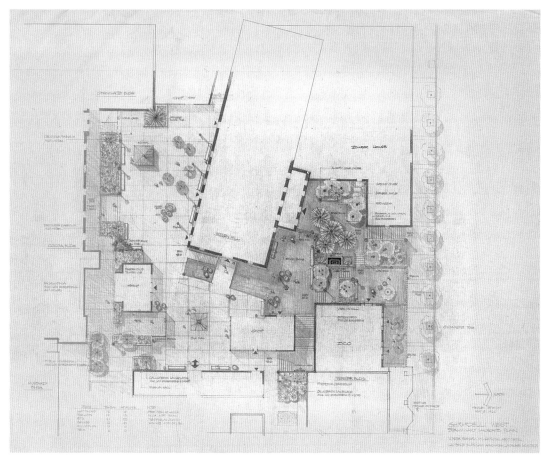

"Ghirardelli West, Preliminary Landscape Plan," 1963. Courtesy LHC.

repurposed in 1967 as "The Cannery." The architect of this even larger retail complex was Joseph Esherick, and Tommy Church was the landscape architect. The scheme featured a large open courtyard with transplanted century-old olive trees.

Following in the original spirit, the adaptive reuse of Ghirardelli Square has itself been adaptively reused and renovated. Fifty years after its opening, few original shops and

Fountain Court, 2013. Photograph by author.

restaurants remain, and as is typical of all commercial districts, users and owners have changed. In the 1980s the gray concrete ground plane was replaced by brick, and a gazebo-like structure by Benjamin Thompson & Associates was added between the plaza and the next level. In the main plaza there are new shops, restaurants, and a children's day care center. Fairmont Heritage Place, a timeshare luxury apartment complex, now occupies the original factory space of the Chocolate, Cocoa, and Mustard Buildings as well as the top floors of the Clock Tower and Woolen Mill Building.

The historic structures are now largely given over to offices and housing that are off-limits to visitors. The grand views to San Francisco Bay remain, but views over the square have been restricted as the upper levels have been privatized and the tiered character of the design experience has been muted. The Fountain Court is still a vibrant tourist attraction and entertainment center.

Ghirardelli Square was honored for its exceptional collaborative achievement among client, architect, and landscape architect. In 1982, less than twenty years after its inception, Ghirardelli Square was added to the National Register of Historic Places, the nation's first major adaptive reuse project.

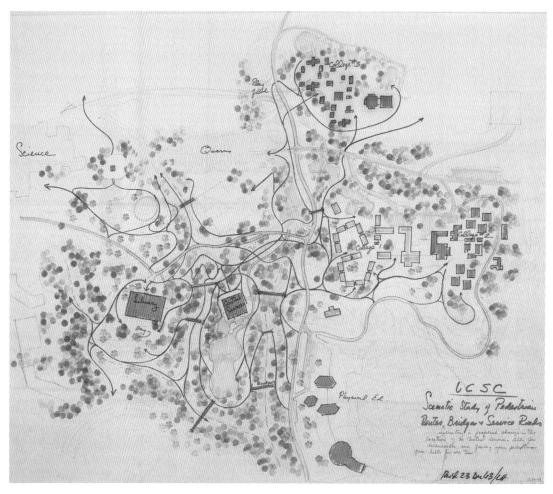

University of California, Santa Cruz, "Schematic Study of Pedestrian Routes, Bridges & Service Roads," drawing, 1963. Courtesy LHC.

UNIVERSITY OF CALIFORNIA, SANTA CRUZ

SANTA CRUZ, CALIFORNIA

1963–1967

The newly established (1965) University of California at Santa Cruz (UCSC) wanted a distinctive campus design to support its innovative educational program of residential colleges, modeled on Oxford and Cambridge. Unlike those urban models, the UCSC colleges were to be embedded in a redwood forest. The entire campus was constructed on a steeply sloping hill, overlooking a grand open meadow, with distant views to the city of Santa Cruz and Monterey Bay.

The campus Master Plan was produced by the team of John Warnecke, Anshen & Allen, Ernest Kump, Theodore Bernardi, and Thomas Church. The university's first chancellor, Dean McHenry, stated that the design of the college must "convey to its members, both students and faculty, a sense of the place which will enhance the educational experience and deepen the cultural implications."[1] The plan was for a system of modestly sized and scaled "cluster colleges" that included residences, dining commons, and classroom spaces. Given the area's amenable climate, the colleges could also partake of the informality of residential design, of living and learning out-of-doors. Thus, in this forested landscape, complexes of buildings were linked by pedestrian pathways and a series of outdoor spaces. Tommy Church remarked that "the buildings are less important in the visual composition than the trees." McHenry noted of Church's contribution that he "has been the main factor in siting every building we have built."[2]

Each college was to have a disciplinary focus: Cowell, the humanities; Crown, the natural sciences; Stevenson, social sciences. Noted Bay Area architects were given commissions for these first three colleges. The character and design of each is distinct, but Halprin, as landscape architect for all three, provided a unifying force by addressing issues related to siting, open space design, and the connections between buildings. Vehicles are kept to the periphery with a drop-off roundabout leading to a gateway and passage into the pedestrian area. The site plan created a compact arrangement of buildings carefully sited and graded to minimize the removal of trees. Masterful site planning addressed the cross section of the slope. Pathways lead walkers up and down, often by the grand curved arcs of baroque steps. (The campus was planned long before the ADA was passed and has only partially been retrofitted.) Halprin designed the connective tissue in this variegated terrain, creating the system of pathways with the bridges traversing the ravines that cut through the campus and service roads that knit the first stage of campus development together.

Courtyards and quadrangles wrap around and frame the existing second-growth redwood groves that tower over the buildings. Each college has two clusters of residence halls enclosing courtyards and a common open space surrounded by classrooms and administration offices, as well as coffee

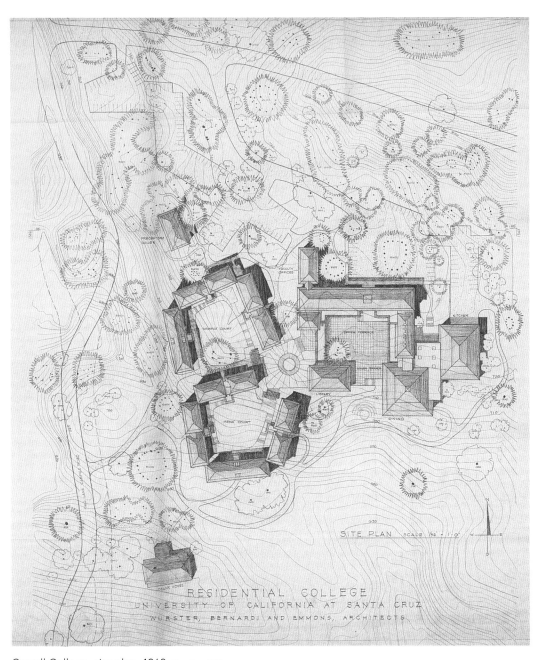

Cowell College, site plan, 1963. Courtesy LHC.

UNIVERSITY OF CALIFORNIA, SANTA CRUZ 121

shops, dining halls, and meeting rooms for student organizations. The residential courtyards are typically located on the slope and the common areas on the flat zones, with the circulation reinforcing the relationships between the units and offering a stimulating variety of interior and exterior views.

A modest scale distinguishes all the buildings with careful attention to the integration of indoor and outdoor spaces, creating both places exposed to the sun and also shaded pockets, and to the variety of hardscape and the softer greener spaces. Cowell College, residential college Number One designed by Wurster, Bernardi & Emmons, set the tone. Located at the ecotone, the transitional area between two communities, the college sits at the edge, overlooking the meadow with the buildings emerging from the forest. Stevenson is adjacent, sharing a dining commons, and is set within the woods, and Crown is located in the nearby forest, up a steep slope.

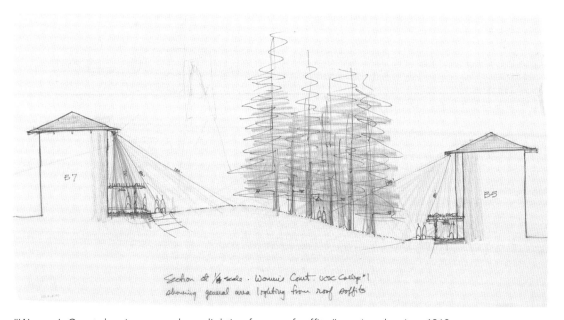

"Women's Court showing general area lighting from roof soffits," section drawing, 1963. Courtesy LHC.

Cowell College, student housing in redwood grove, 2013. Photograph by author.

The residential areas comprised adjacent courtyards for men and women, as campus housing was originally segregated by gender. Now known topographically as the upper and lower quads, at Cowell each features an oval mound across a dramatic twenty-five-foot cross slope. In the upper quad the circumnavigating path passes directly through the redwood grove. The lower courtyard is a simple grass mound with forty-five steps from bottom to top.

At midlevel, between the two quads, is a fountain court. The multiple alternatives of various geometries, pavement patterns, fountain designs, seating possibilities, and tree planting explored for the courtyard are indicative of Halprin's design method. The courtyard functions much like a round-about, a kind of mixing bowl as students move through the college. Surrounded by a ring of pollarded trees, it is now

Cowell College, fountain plaza, 2013. Photograph by author.

adorned with a large mural of "The Maternal Tree." From the court are views out to the meadow.

The fountain court connects to the common area, Cowell's most dramatic feature. This multilevel terraced plaza overlooks the meadow, now dedicated to sport fields, and the Pacific horizon. The lower level is the passage from the dining hall to the fountain court, as well as a stepped amphitheater. A middle level, bounded on two sides by a wisteria arbor and terrace, has tables for study and socializing (the area has been voted the best place to study on campus). The facing building has a second-level loggia over the breezeway entry, a transition between the plaza and the campus forest. The spatial sequence dramatizes moving in and out of the forest, from its shaded canopy into the California sun.

Stevenson (Joseph Esherick, architect) is located on a

small forested knoll. The college has a pair of distinctive interlocking courtyards, one hard-surfaced and containing a single tree, the other built around a compact ring of redwoods with a seating deck located amid the tree trunks. This intimate courtyard with its towering trees is a popular study site. The residential quads located down the slope are hardscaped surfaces, now retrofitted with ramps. The final quad leads to the Stevenson Knoll, a mound crowned by redwoods that offers one of the colleges' most dramatic views. It is a congenial place to study, meet, watch the setting sun, or just be. It epitomizes a site design that capitalizes on the soft rolling topography and the mature trees.

Crown (Ernest J. Kump, architect) is sited on a very steep slope and shares dining with adjacent Merrill, the fourth college to be built. Although the tiled roofs are more

Stevenson College, Knoll, 2013. Photograph by author.

Crown College, steps and path to dormitory, 2013. Photograph by author.

"Californian," and the tighter complex was inspired by Mediterranean villages, the upper and lower quads of the residential buildings feel less connected to the landscape.

Halprin's basic design for these colleges set the pattern and expectation for the university's subsequent campus development, ultimately to ten colleges. Each design displayed careful attention to creating spaces that enriched the college experience and capitalized on the site's qualities. The attention to scale is illustrated by the intimacy of the courtyards, all carefully calibrated in scale from 50 to a maximum of 150 feet across. A rich variety of places were created to address the full range of student life.

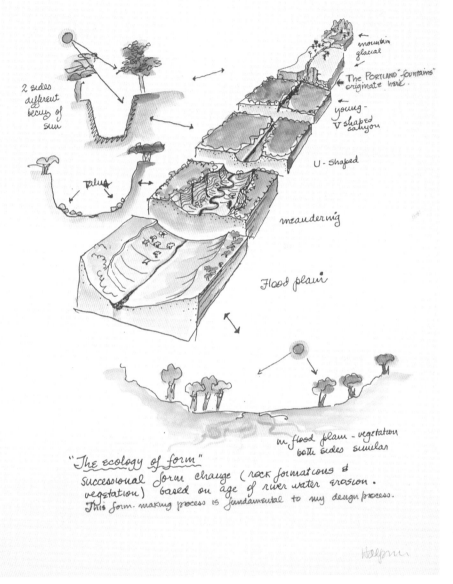

mountain
glacial

The PORTLAND "fountains"
originate here.

2 sides
different
because of
sun

young-
V shaped
canyon

U-shaped

talus

meandering

Flood plain

in flood plain - vegetation
both sides similar

"The ecology of form"
Successional form change (rock formations &
vegetation) based on age of river water erosion.
This form-making process is fundamental to my design process.

Halprin

"The ecology of form," drawing, Portland fountains study, c. 1967. Courtesy LHC.

PORTLAND OPEN SPACE SEQUENCE

PORTLAND, OREGON

1965–1978

In the early sixties an established, historically Jewish neighborhood in South Portland, Oregon, considered a slum by nonresidents, was demolished, and fifty-four city blocks were replaced by Portland Center, the city's first major urban renewal project. The architectural firm SOM designed a mix of high- and low-rise housing knit together by a rich pedestrian system. Working within this milieu, with critical support from Ira Keller, chair of the Portland Development Commission, Halprin created an unprecedented design, an open space sequence punctuated by two dramatic fountains. Simultaneously urban waterfall, plaza, and water garden, they were strikingly imaginative innovations. If the nineteenth-century park was a *rus in urbe,* fragments of rural nature in the city, these were *natura in urbe,* abstractions of a more wild nature in the city. The fountains embodied Halprin's aspiration to create places of performance and a design philosophy that gleaned principles from the natural world but were not meant to mimic or replicate it. In the eight-block open space sequence a tree-lined pedestrian promenade links together Lovejoy Plaza, located in the midst of housing; Forecourt Fountain fronting the Civic Auditorium; and Pettygrove Park, a mounded green interlude between the plazas.

Portland offered Halprin the opportunity to transform his observations of the water and rock "gardens" of the High Sierra into civic spaces.[1] His Sierra drawings were a kind of field research. In them he carefully delineates the shape and edges of streams, ledges above and below water, and the shape and size of rocks, from small stones to boulders. He annotates the drawings with a language of water qualities—turbulence, quiet, trickles, foam, jets, boil, swirls, surge, glide, leap, bubble, flow, and slither—in both words and

Pettygrove Park, 2013. Photograph by author.

Sierra watercourse, drawing, c. 1964. Courtesy LHC.

graphic marks, collections of lines, curves, squiggles, swirls, and arrows of varying lengths and configurations. He notes where solid forms direct the water, shifting its direction and creating eddies, along with pot holes, pools, and weirs. The drawings and words suggest the experience, the sound and feeling, of water. These studies of what he called "the ecology of form" became concept drawings for fountains.

Lovejoy Plaza (1966) was constructed first. With the exception of a small grove and a border of trees, the three-quarter-acre space is paved, a grand environmental sculpture

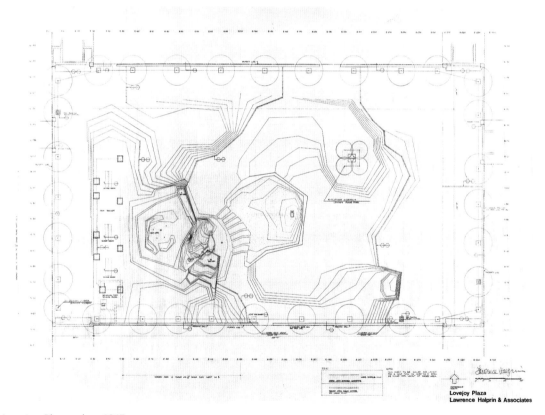

Lovejoy Plaza, plan, 1967. Courtesy LHC.

Lovejoy Plaza, 1985. Photograph by Marc Treib.

of terraced concrete using conventional 2x6s as formwork. Water gardens are analogies of nature, and "The Source," a small fountain constructed south of the plaza in 1968, represents the metaphorical beginning of Halprin's sequence. Along the way, the many properties and expressions of water can be displayed. At Lovejoy, Halprin gave this sequence his personal stamp. The upper section of the plaza is crowned by a structure designed by Charles Moore and William Turnbull. Moore, who was fascinated by water (he had written his dissertation on water and architecture) also worked with Halprin on the fountain.[2] On the upper level a basin collects water that bubbles up from below ground, like a spring. Overflowing the basin it spills into the falls, a cascade of stepped, zigzag, angular forms. The water gushes, sprays, glides, flows, and spurts to the base, where it bubbles and churns, then passes through a series of stepping-stones, from which people can get closer views of the fountain. The water then collects in a large pool that also frames the scene. From the pool, the plaza continues as a series of broad rising and falling concrete steps that complete the space and frame the fountain. As a whole, the plaza can be seen as an angular topographic diagram.

Forecourt Fountain (renamed Ira Keller Fountain in 1978), built four years later, encompasses an entire two-hundred-foot-square city block, framed on three sides by dense plantings of shore pines along berms. Thus it is possible to arrive at the fountain after walking through a miniature, almost bonsai-like, forest. On the fourth side facing the Civic Auditorium (now also named for Keller) the pines frame the falls. From an upper plaza, water emerges from beneath the pavement, as if from under-ground springs. Through channels with pebbled surfaces suggesting tributary streams, the water trickles over small cascades like miniature rapids, to rectilinear platforms and three-foot-deep pools for wading. Then, like a mountain stream, the water abruptly spills over a falls made of great concrete monoliths up to eighteen feet high. Thirteen thousand gallons of water per minute pours in great sheets to a basin below. Dramatic, loud, and mesmerizing, it is an unexpected sight in a city and, like any grand water-fall, demands attention. The fountain faces the auditorium, and from the intervening street side, the plaza steps serve as seating, providing an amphitheater to view the perfor-mance. Overlapping platforms at the base of the falls can function as a stage, but anyone can walk across them and be actors in the drama. Visitors can also walk behind a section of the falls (an idea Halprin developed further in San Francisco's Embarcadero Plaza), and there are steps that recall the region's fish ladders. When the water is turned off, the sculptural forms resemble the base of a Mesoamerican pyramid, although Halprin and Angela Danadjieva, project manager for the design, claimed the mesas and cliffs of the Southwest as well as the waterfalls in the Columbia River Gorge as inspiration. The entire experience is heightened by its urban context. As Halprin wrote in 1963, "Even in a city the sound and sight of water stirs the most elemental and basic roots of our human natures."[3]

Halprin proclaimed the entire progression a micro-

Forecourt Fountain, study model, n.d. Courtesy LHC.

cosm of "what in my view a whole city should be like," and the fountains were hailed as "what may be one of the most important urban spaces since the Renaissance" by Ada Louise Huxtable.[4] Halprin wanted a "people park," and Lovejoy was an immediate success, becoming known nationally as a hippie haven.[5] But without the support of the surrounding commercial district that Halprin had recommended, Lovejoy Plaza fell into disuse and now often sits empty. Nonetheless, it remains a magical design. Halprin revisited Forecourt in 1992 and offered recommendations for its improvement. Observing that the site had become too introverted, he suggested thinning and pruning trees,

Forecourt Fountain, 1970. Courtesy LHC.

Forecourt Fountain, 1985. Photograph by Marc Treib.

restoring night lighting, and planning more cultural activities, as in the park's early years.

The Portland journalist Randy Gragg credits Halprin's design with setting the stage for the city's subsequent development of a system of contemporary parks and plazas. The Halprin Landscape Conservancy, founded in 2001, is dedicated to preserving and maintaining "Portland's greatest living treasure of urban architecture and public space." In 2013 the conservancy spearheaded the successful effort to have the entire Open Space Sequence listed in the National Register of Historic Places.

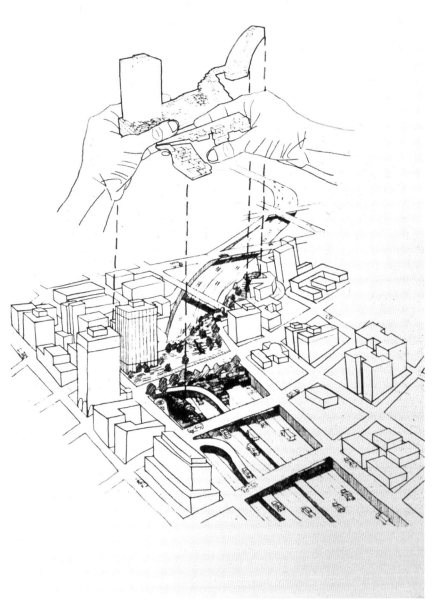

Diagram of Freeway Park over Interstate 5, 1970. Courtesy LHC.

FREEWAY PARK

SEATTLE, WASHINGTON

1970–1976

Seattle Freeway Park leaps over Interstate 5, a daring gesture stitching the city together in the wake of the devastation wrought by the highway construction. In Seattle, Interstate 5, the West Coast route that runs from Canada to Mexico, created a noisy concrete moat separating Downtown from the adjacent residential neighborhood, First Hill. Freeway Park addressed the consequences of the interstate in a way that followed the city's bold tradition of modifying the terrain. Euro-American settlers saw the potential of the site, but they also confronted a topography that would require dramatic transforming to realize it. To build the city, they regraded the land, cutting down hills and using the soil to fill tidal flats and shoreline.

Halprin had consulted with the California Division of Highways on freeways and urban design, topics he elaborated on in his book *Freeways*. He saw freeways as art, the extraordinary engineering feats of western civilization, and as exciting new aspects of the urban experience. But he also bemoaned their devastation of the environment and communities. One ameliorative design response took advantage of air rights to create public space above the freeway. Halprin cited the deck of the Brooklyn Heights promenade, built

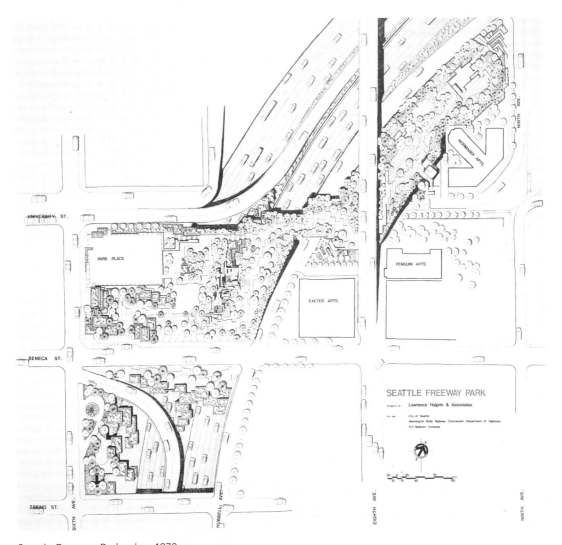

Seattle Freeway Park, plan, 1970. Courtesy LHC.

Park and Interstate 5, 2013. Photograph by Scott Bonjukian. www.thenorthwesturbanist.com

over a multilevel highway in the early fifties, as a prototype. Once again Halprin was a trailblazer. Freeway Park was the first park built over an interstate highway.

As early as 1961, the Seattle architect Paul Thiry had proposed decking I-5, but the deleterious effects of the freeway were not yet understood and the cost was seen as prohibitive.[1] A decade later the original scope of work was limited to treating the freeway border. Halprin, however, through design acumen and deft salesmanship, expanded this minimal expectation into Freeway Park, constructed over ten lanes of traffic, linking upper Downtown and First Hill.[2] At the heart of the park are two water features, Central Plaza Cascade and the Canyon. Like all water features they invite attention—and for Halprin, participation. The Cascade is a series of easily climbed low-level blocks forming a playful wading pool. The unique Canyon, an assembly of giant concrete blocks, is built directly over the highway median, descending to the level of the interstate roadbed. The force of water is palpable, and the sound drowns out the traffic

Union Street entrance stairs and I-5 off-ramp, 2015. Photograph by Scott Bonjukian, www.thenorthwesturbanist.com.

Walkway connecting the park with the Convention Center, 2015. Photograph by
Scott Bonjukian, www.thenorthwesturbanist.com.

noise. People lie on the striated concrete blocks of the canyon, and dangle their feet over the edge, an element of dan-
ger Halprin intended as part of the experience.

The park ascends fifty feet from Downtown, the diverse
elements linked by pathways and steps. From a bird's-eye
view, overlapping hard-surface areas look like giant pavers
extending through the entire 1,300 feet of the original park
(it has since been expanded). The upper section of the park,
on the First Hill side, is a roof garden built over a parking
garage. The original planting suggested a Northwest forest,
an urban oasis set in dramatic contrast to the highway below
and the surrounding city. The grand "roof garden" is a tech-
nical tour de force: there is an intricate irrigation system,
and much of the planting used a lightweight soil mix with
trees in large concrete pots. Just before passing through the

Looking down on the central plaza, 2015. Photograph by Scott Bonjukian, www.thenorthwesturbanist.com.

tunnel beneath the park, drivers have a flashing glimpse of a hanging garden.

Angela Danadjieva, the Halprin associate in charge of the design, brought her Bulgarian stage set and film design background to the project, as she had at Forecourt Fountain. Working out much of the design in clay models, she created a concrete landscape that suggests both the towers and buildings of an urban skyline and a mountainous landscape of precipitous peaks and narrow canyons. The architecture critic Sally Woodbridge declared it "an urban disaster . . . transformed into work of high art." And she predicted that "if all goes well a densely green oasis worthy of nature herself will endure, but only time will tell whether nature is willing to assist man in correcting his mistakes."[3]

International publicity followed Freeway Park's dedication on the Bicentennial July Fourth: this was the first capping of a freeway. After establishing her own firm, Danadjieva twice extended the project, three hundred feet from First Hill to Paul Piggott Corridor in 1984, and five hundred feet back across the interstate to the Washington State Convention Cen-

The Cascade, 1978. Photograph by author.

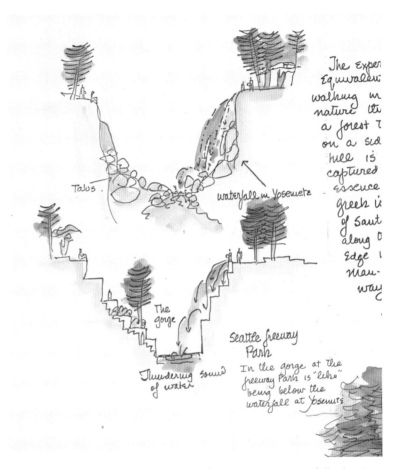

The handwritten annotations on the drawing read:

The Exper[ience] Equivalen[t] walking in nature [in] a forest [or] on a sid[e] hill is captured essence greek i[dea] of Saut[er] along [the] Edge [of a] mau[n]tain way[?]

waterfall in Yosemite

Talus.

The gorge

Thundering sound of water

Seattle freeway Park

In the gorge at the freeway Park is "like" being below the waterfall at Yosemite

The Canyon ("The Gorge") compared to Yosemite waterfall, drawing, detail, n.d. Courtesy LHC.

ter in 1988. Although the extensions added acreage and new linkages, the project's initial success was not repeated. New adjacent buildings now shaded portions of the park, plantings had matured, and what was open and airy became shrouded. A place that had been heralded was ignored and bypassed, as users abandoned the park to a homeless population. Thirty years after the park's dedication, Seattle's Parks and Recreation Department initiated a public planning process to address how to deal with the changes to the park and the culture of the city that supports it. Recommendations included ways to increase activity, access, amenities, and awareness of the park. Most critical was a vegetation management plan that led to a restoration begun in 2006. Thinning was imperative, and had been intended from the outset, and more appropriate plantings were proposed. The changes left the site's "bones" intact, but addressed what Iain Robertson, a University of Washington landscape architect, describes as the "flesh" of the park, the plants. Halprin was brought in to evaluate the new planting proposals and concurred with the recommendations. Although different species were chosen, there was a valiant and successful effort to stay true to the park's original concept, as well as address long-term management concerns. Today, especially as a lunchtime destination, the park is becoming a popular place once again.

Confronted with urban freeways, we have limited choices. We can demolish surface highways and tunnel, as Boston did with its Big Dig, building the Rose Kennedy Greenway on top, or in Seattle, where the Alaska Way viaduct is being replaced. With a sunken highway, the idea presented at Freeway Park—building a cap, lid, or deck over it—became a common model throughout the country. Kanawha Plaza in Richmond, Virginia; Phoenix's Hance Park; River Walk Park in Trenton, New Jersey; Duluth's Leif Erikson Park; and Klyde Warren Park in Dallas have all been built as decks over a freeway. Plans are under discussion in Cincinnati and St. Louis, and in Los Angeles, the city defined by freeways, four such parks are in the planning process. Freeway Park was the beginning.

THE WILLAMETTE VALLEY
CHOICES FOR THE FUTURE

ILLUSTRATED SCENARIOS SHOWING CONSEQUENCES OF ALTERNATIVE APPROACHES TO DEVELOPMENT IN THE VALLEY FOR THE NEXT THIRTY YEARS   AUTUMN 1972

LAWRENCE   HALPRIN   &   ASSOCIATES

The Willamette Valley: Choices for the Future, 1972

THE WILLAMETTE VALLEY: CHOICES FOR THE FUTURE

WILLAMETTE VALLEY, OREGON

1972

In 1970, the year of the first Earth Day, Oregon's governor Tom McCall initiated his Project Foresight. The impetus was an increasing awareness that, continuing unabated growth could destroy the very qualities of the state people valued. Population growth was leading to sprawl and negative impacts on the environment—its quality, water and air pollution, and the loss of agricultural land. The governor's office and the Willamette Valley Environmental Protection and Development Planning Council commissioned the Halprin office to prepare an assessment of alternative futures for the valley. The resulting report was sent to thousands of residents, strategically targeting state legislators, with a cover letter from McCall exhorting readers to think about the future of the valley, home to 70 percent of the state's population. He asked citizens to take their ideas to their representatives and urge new legislation to ensure the continued livability of the state. Thus, *The Willamette Valley: Choices for the Future* played a significant role in a larger story: the planning and policymaking that have guided growth in the Willamette Valley and Oregon state over the past forty years.

The study was presented as an environmental primer, using scenarios as "a way of foretelling the future"—"a new concept and communication method," according to McCall. It was intended not as an explicit plan but as an analysis that would set "the stage for improved citizen involvement and problem identification." The report presented two opposite scenarios for a future beginning in 1982 and ending in 2002. The first projected current trends, the second proposed alternative possibilities. Both addressed seven areas of impact: land use, transportation, open space and recreation, employment and income, pollution, energy and power, and governmental interrelationships.

Scenario One depicted suburban development progressively filling the landscape with houses, roads, cars, and services and causing a decline in urban centers, patchwork development, and a loss of open space. There was a particular concern with visual pollution, what the report called "clutter," a recognition that even if the forces of change were not easily understood, changes in the appearance of the land would be obvious. Illustrated with hand-drawn sketch maps, diagrams, and simple but evocative drawings, the scenario presented change as inexorable unless action was taken. Photographs, especially comparisons with California's Santa Clara Valley, a region that had undergone rampant development, were particularly effective. "Don't Californicate Oregon" bumper stickers had already appeared.

Scenario Two was visionary, but it was not an ecotopian polemic.[1] The report strongly recommended clustered development and contained urban growth, a commonplace in Europe but an anathema in the United States.

1

From World War II the vast majority of Valley residents have depended on their own private automobiles for transportation for any and all purposes--to work, to school, to the shopping center, visiting, and going on vacation. Until the 1970's this auto-dependence did not have a tremendously adverse effect on the environment.

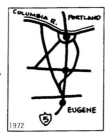

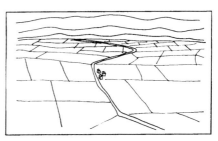

However, the trend continued, and by 1982, the continuing expansion of residential and other developments out further into the countryside was being made more and more possible by new roads of various capacities: local streets, local collectors, arterials, and the connections to existing freeways. Some people were using bus lines.

By 1992, the network of roads, streets, collectors, and arterials had intensified again. To serve the increased population and its vehicles, these systems had to be constantly renewed and upgraded. A lot more land was devoted to the movement and storage of cars. People had to park their cars at home, at work, and anywhere else they took them.

In 2002, a population of 2,500,000 people, most of whom have more than one car per family, really utilizes the increased roadway system of the Valley. Accompanying the spread of houses to the open space and the growth of roads has been the other roadside uses that occur in the suburbs: drive-ins, outdoor movies, shopping centers.

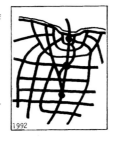

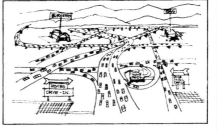

History of regional growth, report, 1972. Author's collection.

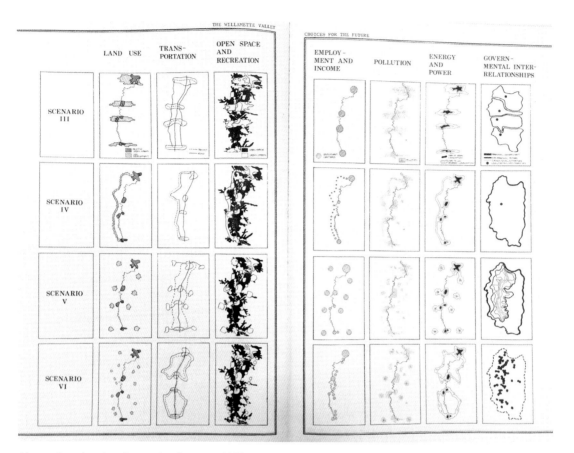

Alternative planning "scenarios," report, 1972. Author's collection.

The state mandated urban growth boundaries the following year, and while not as successfully as people had hoped, sprawl has generally been contained. The resulting increase in urban density has largely benefited community life. The central role of transportation in determining the pattern of development was acknowledged in a proposal for a valleywide elevated rail mass transit system and recommendations for clustering developments around transit (a forerunner of the now-common practice of Transit Oriented

Development). Neither came to pass, and a high-speed rail link in the valley has been under discussion ever since. In Portland, however, an integrated mass transit system of light rail, streetcars, and buses was constructed. The idea of a Willamette River Greenway was endorsed, a program that was established in 1967 and legislated in 1973.

The report was accompanied by a slide show prepared by the Halprin office that they presented at 275 public meetings attended by more than twenty thousand people. The report and the meetings were promotional devices to help enact groundbreaking land use regulations. In lauding Halprin's legacy, the Portland journalist Randy Gragg has noted that "enough Oregonians saw the study to help propel the key piece of legislation, Senate Bill 100," passed in 1973.[2] The bill placed the state at the forefront of national land-use planning.[3] While economic development was to be supported, growth was to be managed and prime farmland and the environment protected. Consistent with the spirit inherent in the Project Foresight process, the goal of managing growth addressed citizen involvement, a fundamental element in *The Willamette Valley: Choices for the Future*. As the Oregon planner Steven Ames has remarked, "More than planners, all Oregonians owe a debt of gratitude to Halprin for his clarion call at a pivotal moment in our history."[4]

Franklin Delano Roosevelt Memorial, aerial view, 2011. Photograph by Carol M. Highsmith. Courtesy CHA.

FRANKLIN DELANO ROOSEVELT MEMORIAL

WASHINGTON, DC

1974–1997

For Halprin the significance of being chosen to design the Franklin Delano Roosevelt Memorial was deeper than the dramatic civic and patriotic aspect of the work. The honor was personal, for like many people of his generation he revered FDR. Congress had authorized a memorial in 1955 and in 1959 had chosen the site on the Tidal Basin. Two design competitions were held, but in both, the winning design failed to gain sufficient institutional support. Halprin had entered the second competition with the architect Minoru Yamasaki, and his 1960 Notebooks show the germ of his concept of a spatial progression.[1] More than a decade later, in 1974, Halprin was selected from a short list of seven designers to undertake the memorial (the support of Oregon senator Mark Hatfield, an admirer of Halprin's work in Portland, was crucial). The design was substantially completed by 1978, but construction did not begin until 1991. The memorial was finally dedicated in 1997.

155

The FDR Memorial is sited between the Jefferson and the 2011 Martin Luther King Jr. memorials, with the spire of the Washington Monument across the basin commanding the view. In this ceremonial ensemble, the FDR Memorial is out of sight. Hidden behind the cherry trees that encircle the basin, it does not have the grand, beckoning presence of the other presidential memorials. Rather, Halprin created a passage that must be entered and walked through to be fully experienced, a progression through four "rooms" representing FDR's four terms as president. They highlight the man, the times, and the accomplishments of his tenure in office in ways that are instructional, inspirational, and symbolic in varying degrees—a spatial, temporal, and historical narrative, or in Halprin's words, an "experiential history lesson."[2]

"I thought of the wall in musical terms and studied the elevations in model form as if they were made up of notes on a page," he explained.[3] The memorial is composed much

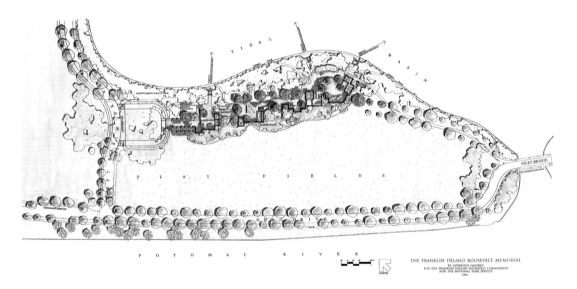

Plan, 1995. Courtesy Steven Koch.

like a symphony, a score with four movements. The "instruments" of the narrative are a design vocabulary of granite blocks, water, sculpture, space, and FDR's words, each playing their part. From its earliest stages, every aspect of the project was studied in meticulous detail through the development of large models and full-scale mock-ups. He chose the sculptors by working with them on what he called "jam sessions," a Take Part process that set the stage for their collaborations. Halprin's use of text and figurative sculpture was in the conservative tradition of commemorative statuary, but here encapsulated in a modernist design framework.[4]

The entire memorial encompasses seven and a half acres. The passage through the rooms is eight hundred feet long, a string of loosely structured courtyards that open to a park-like setting just above the shoreline of the basin. A parallel path along the basin gives glimpses of the memorial through the gnarled cherry trees and granite seating niches. Allowing

FRANKLIN DELANO ROOSEVELT
PRESIDENT OF THE UNITED STATES
1933 – 1945

Bird's-eye view of the memorial. Courtesy Steven Koch.

Memorial at dusk. Photograph by Carol M. Highsmith. Courtesy CHA.

moments of repose, it is also a place for contemplation and respite.

In response to objections from the disability community that the memorial failed to acknowledge FDR's polio, a life-size statue of Roosevelt seated in his wheelchair—a view he did not want photographed during his presidency—was added to the original entry. Although Halprin initially protested the addition, he ultimately deftly orchestrated the location and the selection of the sculpture, so it fits seamlessly into the original design and concept.[5] Behind FDR is a quotation from Eleanor Roosevelt, attesting to the fact that her husband's struggle with polio is what prepared him for the hardships that were to come. The word "Prologue," engraved in the pavement, suggests that this moment not only precedes his presidency but also begins a story. This space, an enclosed court with four tiers of pink Carnelian granite set within a lush planting has a quiet gran-

Carving stone during construction. Photograph by Carol M. Highsmith. Courtesy CHA.

"The Rural Couple" and "Depression Breadline," bronze statues by George Segal, 1991. Photograph by Carol M. Highsmith. Courtesy CHA.

deur and sets the stage for the spatial narrative. A wall of water and the first of twenty-eight aphoristic writings greet the visitor.

One side of the memorial is a continuous twelve-foot-high wall of four tiers of granite blocks (most are actually stone veneer) that frame the four rooms. The opposite border is densely planted, with periodic openings giving views to the Tidal Basin. On the other side of the wall is a recreational park, what Halprin called the profane space opposing the memorial's sacred space. "I pledge you, I pledge myself, to a New Deal for the American People" is inscribed on the memorial wall, together with a relief of the presidential seal. A quotation from a campaign address follows: "In these days of difficulty we Americans everywhere must and shall choose the path of social justice . . . the path of faith, the path of hope and the path of love toward our fellow men." The words introduce the passage through the memorial and also suggest a direction to follow to live up to Roosevelt's legacy. The quote is adjacent to a frieze by Robert Graham of FDR waving to the crowds and the classic words from his first inaugural address: "The only thing we have to fear is fear itself."

The story of the Great Depression follows with life-size sculptures by George Segal. They include a man listening to Roosevelt's "Fireside Chat" on the radio, an Appalachian farm couple, and a breadline of five men, all with despondent expressions. Visitors can interact with the sculptures, taking a place on the breadline or next to the couple, to

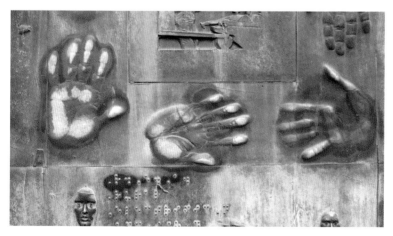

"Social Programs," detail, bronze panels by Robert Graham, 1997. Photograph by author, 2013.

photograph themselves with these iconic Depression images, perhaps imagining themselves in their circumstance. The sculptures put a face on the Depression and pose questions to those unfamiliar with the images.

On the opposite side of the Great Depression wall is an outdoor room dedicated to FDR's second term, which describes the multiple accomplishments of the New Deal, the domestic highlight of his presidency. Five sculptural columns by Robert Graham are printing drums used to make the imprints on the facing wall which display iconic aspects of New Deal programs, along with individual faces. This section is the most didactic. It is necessary to get very close to the grid of images to read or see most of them, thus both columns and their imprints invite touching, and the lower courses are now burnished. A stepped waterfall frames the wall and evokes dams constructed by the TVA—the water cascades, then stops, then flows again. Water was a characteristic element in Halprin's design palette, and in a sense the memorial is a great water garden. Halprin explained and perhaps rationalized its use here by connecting it thematically to FDR's life and work, but it also serves the practical purpose of screening the noise from nearby Ronald Reagan Airport.

When visitors enter the third room, the room of war, they encounter his proclamation: "We must be the arsenal of democracy" on the wall, and a passage through blocks of stone is inscribed with FDR's exclamation, "I hate war." The fallen, broken, and scattered stones are displaced from the exterior wall that seems to collapse, and water flows through its shattered structure, as if coursing through the ruins of a city. Neil Estern's sculpture of FDR seated with his cape wrapped around his body comes into view. At nine feet, the stature is relatively close to human scale and approachable,

FDR and his dog Fala, 2006. Sculpture by Neil Estern. Photograph by Carol M. Highsmith. Courtesy CHA.

unlike those of Jefferson and Lincoln. His pose is grand, yet his dog Fala is by his side. Individuals and families have their portraits taken *with* Roosevelt, and many visitors hold his hand, which was soon burnished after the dedication. Children sit in his lap, pose, and play with Fala. A closer look reveals the sculpted wheel of his chair beneath his cape. The entire ensemble reflects the intimacy Halprin's generation felt toward FDR.

FDR's fourth term was truncated: he died just before the end of the war. The quiet space of this room is introduced by a sculptural frieze of his funeral cortège by Leonard Baskin, which sits above a still pool. A statue of Eleanor Roosevelt stands in the room. Her statement in the prologue introduces the memorial, and her presence here is a fitting conclusion. A fifth course has been added to the stone wall, suggest-

Waterfall and cherry trees, 2011. Photograph by Carol M. Highsmith. Courtesy CHA.

Waterfall. Photograph by Carol M. Highsmith. Courtesy CHA.

ing the future and Roosevelt's legacy—the nation resting on the foundation his presidency established. A final dramatic water wall, cascading over stones, and regathering, images the building of a nation, a democracy, and suggests that the story—the task—is unfinished. Engraved on the stone wall is the final quotation: the Four Freedoms.

In the Park @
Levi Strauss
Aug 16, 1978

Halprin

"In the Park @ Levi Strauss," drawing, August 16, 1978. Courtesy LHC.

LEVI STRAUSS PLAZA

SAN FRANCISCO, CALIFORNIA

1978–82

Nestled at the foot of San Francisco's iconic Telegraph Hill and located only blocks from both the original and the later Halprin offices is Levi Strauss Plaza. Framed on one side by the hill and by San Francisco Bay on the other, the plaza can be entered from many points along the adjoining streets, but those who climb down the steps of Telegraph Hill are rewarded with a spectacular view of the bay with the plaza in the foreground.

Halprin had a long relationship with the Haas family, prominent philanthropic pillars of the San Francisco community and owners of one of the state's venerated enterprises, Levi Strauss & Co. He designed private gardens for family members in the 1950s, as well as projects bearing their name in Israel, notably the Haas Promenade. In his first sketches Halprin made notes of a plaza between the corporate buildings as a place of "mts.-grottos-falls." In a subsequent drawing he labeled it a "3 dimensional collage – water

– planting." The project is divided by Battery Street into two segments, a hard-surfaced plaza bounded by angular red brick buildings and a green pastoral park. There is a vitalizing duality to the design, in both function and form, yet the park and plaza are deftly united. Both sections feature water gardens, but of strikingly different types. The water source in each is a grand fountain where water emerges from stone.

In the plaza, a huge block of carnelian granite quarried from Halprin's beloved High Sierra is a dramatic sculptural statement. Water cascades from an invisible source on top of the stone over the lip of the monolith and tumbles in a cacophonous display over steps, fills basins, forms pools, and

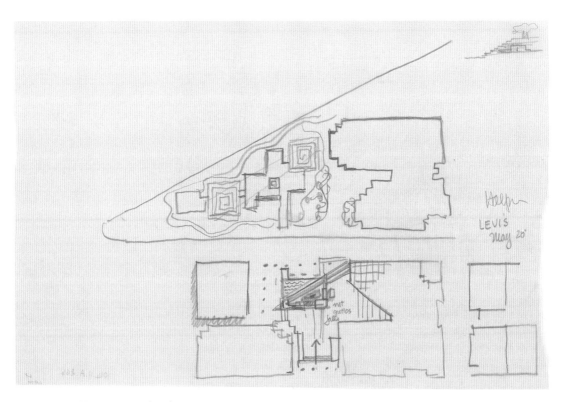

"Levi's, May 28," concept sketch. Courtesy LHC.

surrounds circular concrete pads to disappear finally into a swirling vortex fronting the monolith, a perfect circle set against the almost cubic stone.

The plaza is laid out in a pattern of white *X*'s set within a grand grid of brick-lined squares on top of a gray concrete slab. The *X*'s echo the zigzag stepped pattern of the Levi Strauss Corporate Headquarters designed by HOK and Gensler + Associates. The bold ground plane extends across the street into the adjacent park space before giving way to the sinuous curves of the park—a simple yet daring transition. Although the plaza and park appear to be public, they are meticulously maintained private properties.

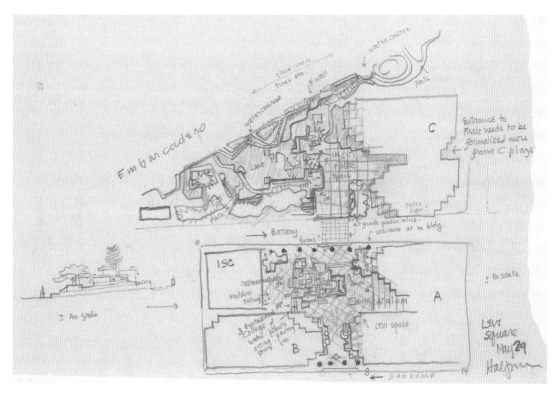

"Levi Square, May 29," concept sketch. Courtesy LHC.

The park area is a modern California version of a Japanese stroll garden. An architectonic waterfall cascades into a pool with stepping stones before draining into a highly stylized stream running through a green meadow. The urban creek wraps around a willow island, flows beneath a small bridge, and then disappears into a culvert, appearing to pass beneath the Embarcadero, whose multiple lanes

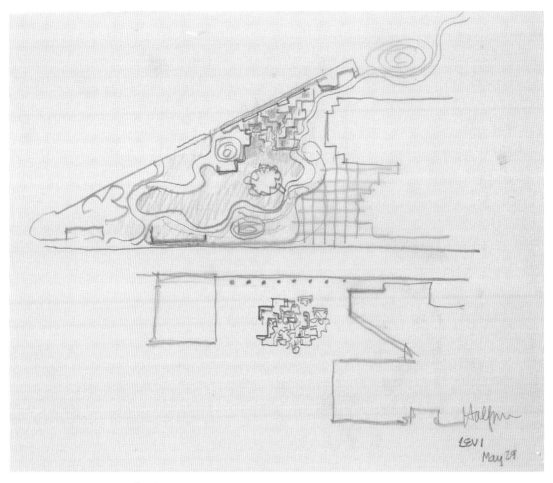

"Levi, May 29," concept sketch. Courtesy LHC.

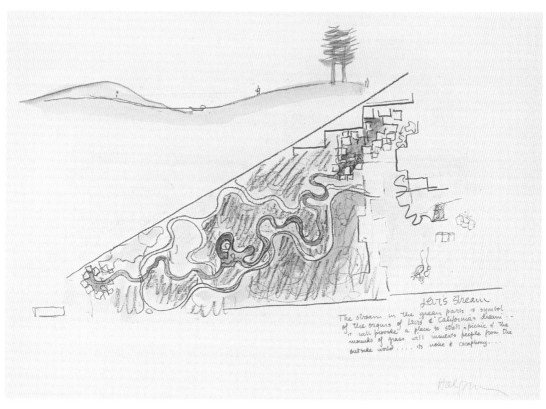

The stream in the green park is symbol of the origins of Levi's & California's dream... it will provide a place to stroll, picnic & the mounds of grass will insulate people from the outside world.... its noise & cacophony...

Levi's stream

"Levi's stream," concept sketch, detail. Courtesy LHC.

of traffic cut off direct access to the bay, truncating what should be a natural link. The stream is bordered by weeping willows, with intermittent granite boulders and stepping stones across the water. A cobblestone-edged pathway through the area has matured into passages of shaded walk along the stream, surrounded by sunny mounds, both welcome aspects in San Francisco's variable climate. The final design compresses and abstracts the course of water from mountains to upland meadows and ultimately to the sea.[1] Halprin viewed it as a narrative of the Levi Strauss story, the fountains and streams a metaphor for the Sierra and the

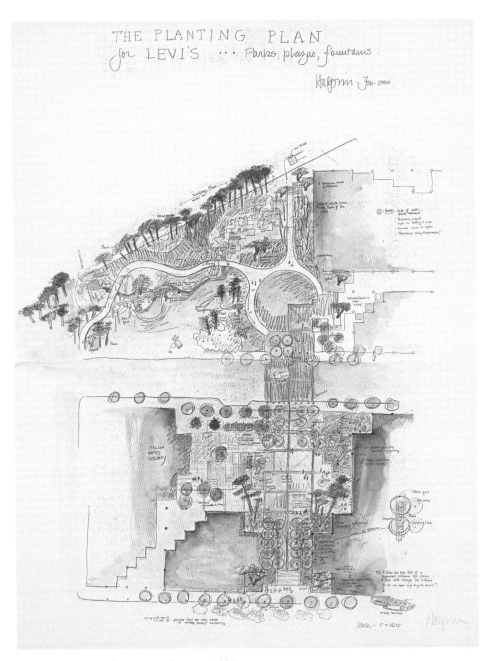

"The Planting Plan for Levi's," drawing, 1980. Courtesy LHC.

California Gold Rush, when Strauss founded the company and helped build the new city, and the plaza representing the present day.

The project exemplifies Halprin's distinctive use of materials, drawing attention to the qualities of stone, concrete, and water to create a refined design language. The stones change from rough boulders that look randomly placed on the grassy mounds and in the watercourse to quarried blocks along the pathways which double as seating. Similarly, concrete evolves from rough to smooth to polished. A signature of many of Halprin designs, the interaction of water with a variety of surfaces is also featured. There are cultural allusions as well, to an Italian piazza on the one hand and to a Japanese garden on the other,

Stream through park, 2013. Photograph by author.

View to Telegraph Hill. Photograph by Tara C. Robinson.

"The Levi Strauss Park," drawing, August 17, 1978. Courtesy LHC.

an astute gesture acknowledging the city's ethnic history. There is a studied placement of benches, lighting, and simple stone slabs and walls that serve as boundaries; seating, platforms, and stages invite sitting, reclining, and performing. There are subtle transitions, from street to plaza to park and paths and walkways to green grass, where the looped walk surrounds the stream and mounds.

The planting design includes a sycamore allée entry and willows along the watercourses. Bordering the plaza, plantings reveal the influence of Christopher Tunnard's 1938 *Gardens in the Modern Landscape,* essays that had had

Stepping stones, Levi Strauss Plaza. Photograph by Tara C. Robinson.

such a formative impact on Halprin as a student. Tunnard observed that dramatizing the sculptural qualities of plant materials was one of the distinguishing characteristics of modern landscape design and suggested that Asian, particularly Japanese, influence was equally characteristic. Both qualities are clearly manifest at Levi Strauss Plaza.

Children especially revel in the stepping-stones that are invitations to explore, and for them a bit of a challenge, a performance Halprin certainly intended. In fact, much of the park functions as a de facto playground, although the overall feeling is of an oasis adjacent to the rush of traffic and busy promenade along the Embarcadero. The two sections, plaza and park, are distinctive, but together they achieve a balance—simultaneously corporate and public, playful and contemplative, active and passive.

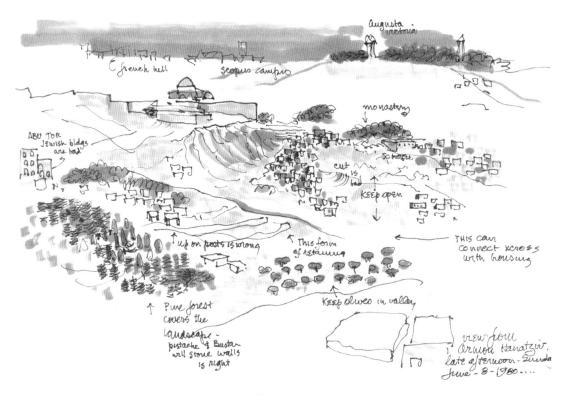

"View from Armon Hanatziv, late afternoon," drawing, June 8, 1980. Courtesy LHC.

THE HAAS PROMENADE AND THE RICHARD AND RHODA GOLDMAN PROMENADE

JERUSALEM

1984–2002

At Armon Hanatziv in Jerusalem, Halprin created a design of lasting significance that embodied his philosophy and demonstrated his insight into Israeli culture. Comprising a hill and ridge south of the Old City overlooking the Kidron Valley, Armon Hanatziv is the New Testament Hill of Evil Counsel, which included the site of the British High Commissioner's residence during the Mandate, and later the United Nations Headquarters (1948–67). Jerusalem sits at a spatial and temporal ecotone on the cusp of the desert, at the intersection of green trees and sand, and at the meeting place of ancient and contemporary worlds. To the west are the city's newer neighborhoods, to the east, ancient villages. The associations of the site touch on the history of the Abrahamic religions and the modern history of the region. From Armon Hanatziv, the views are spectacular. In the foreground, the village of Silwan; at the center, the sacred core of the Old City of Jerusalem with the brilliant golden Dome of the

Rock; and surrounding, the hilltops including the Mount of Olives and Mount Scopus. In Halprin's first notes he was taken by the "incredible view—perhaps the most awe inspiring urban view in the world . . . There is a quality of ageless urban/landscape quality that is ineffable—the city and the landscape make an organic whole inseparable . . . the view *must* be kept in our planning for the entire area—not only the ridge but the slopes . . . great promenade is enuf—a great piece of theater!"[1] These initial ideas—the spectacular view and the theatrical aspect, where all visitors are actors in the performance—remained paramount throughout the project.

The first phase, the Haas Promenade (1984) designed by Halprin and Shlomo Aronson, was extended into a second phase by Aronson's design for the Gabriel Sherover (1989) and Trottner (1990) Promenades. The Richard and Rhoda Goldman Promenade (2002) by Halprin and Bruce Levin extended the project to the two-and-a-half-kilometer-long complex that Halprin had envisioned, known simply as "the Tayelet." There is a continuity to the whole, yet each section is distinct. The *tayelet* is a distinct Israeli landscape type with elements of the Mediterranean *corso*, urban boulevard, waterfront promenade, and garden belvedere. They are grand terraces that connect the built environment to its larger context, urban living rooms, and meeting grounds where people gather. There are notable *tayelot* in Tel Aviv, Haifa, and Netanya.

The Haas Promenade is literally a grand belvedere, offering a beautiful view preceded by a carefully calibrated sequence leading toward it. Most visitors arrive by car or bus, so the road and parking are screened variously by a planted buffer, lawn, walls, and seating. The walkway is a wide expanse of creamy limestone—the required facade material for all structures in Jerusalem. The path is bounded

Haas Promenade, 2011. Photograph by author.

by a low seating wall with a metal railing, punctuated by light posts and rounded capstones. From below, the entire promenade reveals itself to be an arched wall, which at its base gives way to a lawn, groves of olive and cypress, and pathways snaking through the valley. The land is the shape of a grand amphitheater accentuated by the great arc of the promenade, a form repeated in a lower belvedere that thrusts out from the walkway.

The design derives from multiple sources revealed in Halprin's Notebooks, including ancient works, traditional practices, and the designs of the British romantic period

in Mandatory Palestine. The arches of the wall intention-
ally recall the structure of the aqueducts that in ancient
times brought water to the city from the south. Halprin
carefully analyzed both the vernacular methods of stone
construction and detailing that characterize the Old City,
and the buildings constructed during the British Mandate.
His detail studies of the YMCA (1933), designed by Arthur
Loomis Harmon, led to the rounded capstones along the
seating wall of the Tayelet. Halprin's passion for the stones
of Jerusalem is apparent throughout. The stones ascend,
in classical fashion, from rough lower courses to smooth

Belvedere, Haas Promenade, clay model, 1986. Courtesy LHC.

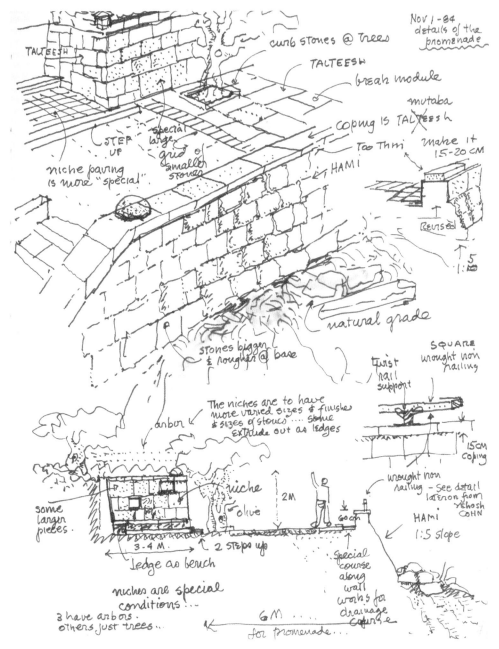

Nov 1-84
details of the
promenade

TALTEESH

curb stones @ trees

TALTEESH

break module

mutaba

coping is TAL~~TEE~~sh

Too Thin

make it
15-20 CM

REVISED

STEP
UP

special
large
grid of
smaller
stones

niche paving
is more "special"

HAMI

5
1:___

natural grade

stones bigger
& rougher @ base

SQUARE
wrought iron
railing

twist
rail
support

15 CM
coping

The niches are to have
more varied sizes & finishes
& sizes of stones .... some
extrude out as ledges

arbor

niche

olive

2 M

wrought iron
railing - see detail
later on from
Yehosh
COHN

some
larger
pieces.

60 cm

HAMI
1:5 slope

3-4 M

2 steps up

ledge as bench

niches are special
conditions ...

3 have arbors.
others just trees ...

6 M ....

for promenade...

special
course
along
wall
works for
drainage
course

"Details of the promenade," drawing, November 1, 1984. Courtesy LHC.

surfaces. The metalwork derives from traditional ironwork found in the city. While the sources may be apparent to some observers, the design is not a pastiche but asserts a unique identity.

Halprin initially conceived of the project as stretching from the neighborhood of Abu Tor south of the Old City to the forested area beneath the United Nations Headquarters, over two kilometers. The Haas Promenade was the first phase and is the hinge between the two subsequent sections, the Sherover Promenade, which extends north to Abu Tor, and the Trottner Promenade, a pathway on the slopes below. A dramatic stairway to a shaded belvedere leads to pathways offering a stunning assemblage of iconic elements of the Israeli landscape, with olive groves and wheat fields. The grand view is still of the valley and the Old City but now also up toward the Haas Promenade, which crowns the brow of the hill.

For the final phase of the project, the Richard and Rhoda Goldman Promenade, Halprin collaborated with Bruce Levin, who had worked for him before making *aliyah* (immigrating to Israel) and establishing his own firm. The design of this section links it to the east end of the Haas Promenade. An entry fountain leads to pathways through a seventy-five-year-old Keren Kayemet (Jewish National Fund) pine forest, below the UN Headquarters. Remnants of the British High Commissioner's residence and terraced garden are incorporated into the design. From the inception of the project Halprin spoke of creating a "townscape" promenade, not a "gardenesque" one. At the Goldman Promenade, he employed Gordon Cullen's townscape method of using sequential drawings to analyze a place and then propose design alternatives.

Much of the project was designed in the field. Levin

reports that here "Larry put his ego aside and let the site dictate the design similar to his work at the Yosemite Falls trail . . . the design of the Goldman was determined by the pine grove, and sprinkling of minor 'Belvederes' where great view vistas open to the Temple Mount, and the Judean Desert. We literally walked the site in slow motion, every 20 yards stopping, discussing, Larry sketching trees and stones and jotting the ideas in his notebook. For me it was amazing to see how a landscape architect could let the design flow out of the site itself. I think that few if any architects today have the patience, connection to the land—the site."[2]

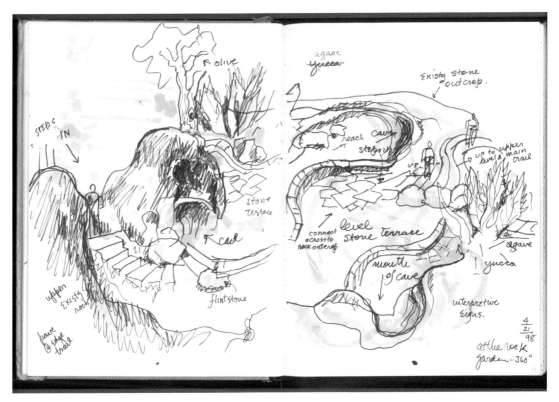

"At the Rock Garden–360°," drawing, April 21, 1998. Courtesy LHC.

The inspiration of the "incredible view" remained paramount. Halprin's drawings illustrate the desired effect, with particular attention to elements that were to be retained, accentuated, or removed. As late as 2000, days before the

"Plan at rock garden area," drawing, 1997. Courtesy Bruce Levin.

Goldman Promenade pathways, 2009. Photograph by author.

Second Intifada, Halprin was personally selecting stones from a quarry on the West Bank. Levin notes that "Halprin saw the personal visit to the quarry and architect's stone selection as an essential and personal involvement essential in his role as landscape creator."[3] The path culminates at a stone amphitheater with views back to the Old City and east to the Dead Sea, Jordan, and the mountains of Edom in the distance.

The performance of the Tayelet has multiple dimensions, and the design sums up many of Halprin's concerns and passions—community, movement and choreography, and the method and meaning of the RSVP cycles. The ultimate goal is the "performance," how it enriches people's experience of places and interactions with each other. Halprin's Jerusalem drawings highlight the relationship between places, noting not only what is visible, but what is beyond the visual field and yet an equal part of the design. This holistic philosophy is nowhere more apparent than in his understanding of Armon Hanatziv, a place that is both prospect and refuge, a viewpoint from which one can take in the magnificent scene from the safety of distance. The view affords a maplike overview and, as such, is an aid to understanding this com-

View from Goldman to Haas Promenade, drawing, 1997. Courtesy Bruce Levin.

plex landscape. The hill is a place from which to put things into perspective, where people point, identify, and learn the landscape.

The site has become a mandatory destination for all visitors to Jerusalem. The panoramic view almost demands interpretation, explanation, and personal reflection. It is where a guide, a friend, or a family member recounts a history, one that can span the ancient to the modern. It is common to hear stories—"When I was a child the city ended over there" . . . "In '48 we moved from there" . . . "During the intifada, this is where . . ."—or tales from the Bible, or the anticipation of what peace would look like. It is a great amphitheater space, a *teatro mundi*. The collective design at Armon Hanatziv befits its honored situation. The design embraces the landscape, where the weight of history, faith, and daily life occupy equal status.

This has to be the width
of the VIEW corridor as
seen from N. side drive

these cedars
should be
removed

lower
falls

oak

OAKS

present
cable
line

Tlurlp?

5/11

4
14
02

Yosemite, view corridor, drawing, April 14, 2002. Courtesy LHC.

YOSEMITE FALLS TRAIL

YOSEMITE VALLEY, CALIFORNIA

1997–2005

In 1863 Frederick Law Olmsted went west to assume a posi-
tion with the Mariposa Mining Corporation, and on his
first visit to Yosemite discovered the "union of the deepest sublimity with the deepest beauty of nature."[1] Olmsted
described the valley as a "chasm" and the Merced River,
which flows through the valley floor, as "a broad stream of
the clearest water, rippling over a pebbly bottom, and eddy-
ing among banks of ferns and rushes; sometimes narrowed
into sparkling rapids and sometimes expanding into placid
pools which reflect the wondrous heights on either side."[2]
His prescient 1865 report on managing the site anticipated
millions of visitors. To handle them, Olmsted advised building a looped road in the valley and from it paths to viewing
points.

More than a century later Halprin was commissioned
to redesign one such path, the route that leads to the base of
Yosemite Falls, at 2,425 feet, the tallest waterfall in North

America. This rare late-in-life opportunity allowed Halprin to return to the Sierra landscape that played such a significant role in his life as well as a chance to work in one of the nation's sacred natural sites, and the most visited site in the park. As Halprin associate Paul Scardina succinctly noted, "They gave us the Hope Diamond to polish."[3]

Confronting Halprin and his design team at this glorious site were a congested fume-filled parking lot, unsightly facilities, and a deteriorated, crowded asphalt path. Halprin hosted two "Take Part" workshops to reach a consensus about how to proceed. The stakeholders asked to participate included National Park Service personnel and members of the Yosemite Conservancy, a nonprofit group that raised most of the funds for the $13.5 million project.[4]

The Yosemite plan was largely created through sketches in the field, using the townscape method Halprin employed so successfully at the Goldman Promenade in Jerusalem. His method, which suggests choreography, also has affinities with film editing. In the manipulation of the pathway design, Halprin created a rhythm, while orchestrating views of the falls. Both the visual and kinesthetic experience of the sequential progression and measured passage to the falls suggest points to pause and contemplate (or photograph) the dramatic scenery. It is as if Halprin had internalized his systematic motation studies.

Halprin's path begins with a small informal stone amphitheater near the site of the Indian village of Koomine. The previous route to the falls had no defined edges or rest areas, and visitors often wandered off the designated path, compromising the natural habitat. Halprin bordered the trail with low stone walls that funnel visitors to the path and align their attention toward the falls. The demarcation of the trail was essential both to direct visitors and to protect the sur-

Walkway to falls, 2008. Photograph by Daniel K. Horner.

rounding landscape. (The eastern loop and the trail were made ADA compliant with the exception of several yards leading to the main terrace.) Halprin realized that the final destination did not need to be reached instantly and created a more meandering route than the original straight walk. He removed and thinned trees and placed fallen logs to alter views or limit access.

Halprin created a typology of Yosemite stones—boulders in walls, freestanding boulders, stacked stones, and flat stones—and related them to human scale. In his notations and drawings he characterized the sculptural qualities of each type and size of stone. Halprin's sequential drawings

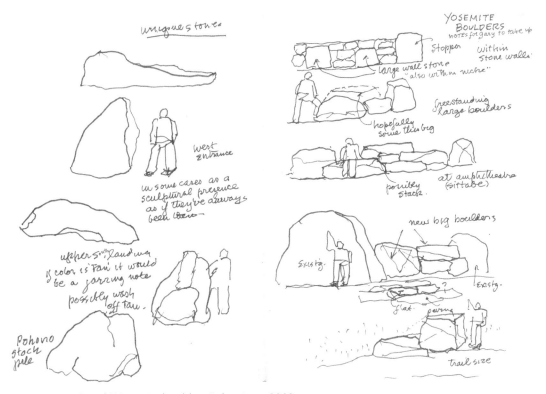

"Unique stones" and "Yosemite boulders," drawings, 2003. Courtesy LHC.

Viewing area and bridge, model, 2001. Courtesy LHC.

View terrace, 2013. Photograph by author.

Rest area along pathway, 2013. Photograph by author.

carefully note existing stones, those to be removed, and the
location and type of stones to be added. The 1,893 tons of
granite for the stonework came from a nearby quarry or
were recycled from the park. The construction was carried
out by QuarryHouse and its master stonemason, Ed West-
brook, who would go on to work at Stern Grove. Details are
in sympathy with Civilian Conservation Corps work of the
1930s.[5]

During construction, Halprin supervised the placement
of individual stones with a deliberation reminiscent of that
used to select symbolic stones in Chinese, Korean, and Japanese gardens. A grouping of existing large boulders form
part of the entry gate to the pathway. He created borders and
seating areas that resonate with the grand granite monoliths
framing the valley and forming the spillway for the falls. The

Lower Yosemite Falls viewing terrace was expanded, and the sharp angles of the pavers are deftly fitted against boulders that meld into the scree at the base of the falls. These are stone gardens, recalling the inspiration for his art that Halprin described in his early articles "The Gardens of the High Sierra" and "The Shape of Erosion."

From the primary viewing area Halprin's path crosses a bridge that is sprayed with mist from the falls during spring. It leads to a looped walk constructed with the informal rustic character of Yosemite's wilderness trails. The path wraps around great boulders and through the forest, crossing the braided meandering course of Lower Yosemite Creek. Dry

Halprin sketching on the ADA Trail, 2005. Courtesy LHC.

"Yosemite, on the ADA trail. The big rock," drawing, 2005. Courtesy LHC.

"On the ADA trail. The big rock," June 27, 2013. Photograph by author.

in winter, in spring its banks overflow, so sections of the path become a raised wooden walkway. Four reconstructed bridges and one new bridge cross the creek as they intersect with the path. Other stones are the supports for orientation and directional signs. The new loop has three main entry points, including one of the valley's shuttle bus stops, featuring six battered granite stone piers supporting the roof, designed in concert with the trail.

The design for Yosemite Falls encourages lingering, learning, and experiencing the dramatic surroundings. Human intervention into such a landscape could be interpreted as an encroachment, but Halprin's design has modesty, expressing a level of restraint and maturity in the face of grand, sublime forces. The design epitomizes Halprin's philosophy, inspired by the Sierra: "Studying the granite formations, rivers, lakes and waterfalls and their evolution has formed the basis of my design philosophy. I learned not to copy the forms of nature but to understand the processes by which natural forms arise."[6]

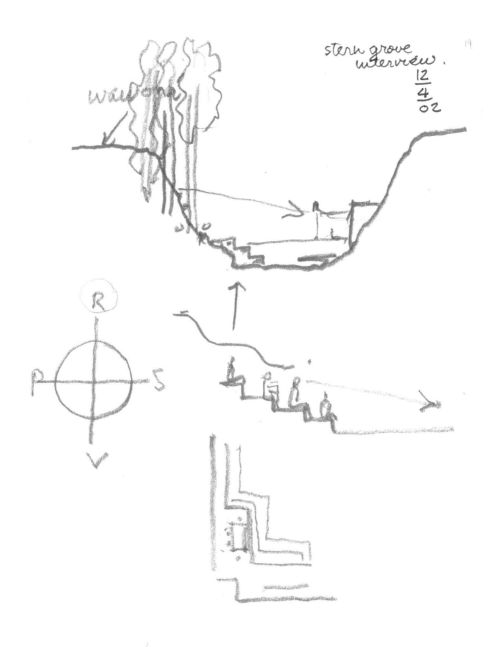

"Stern Grove interview," December 4, 2002. Courtesy LHC.

SIGMUND STERN
RECREATION GROVE

SAN FRANCISCO, CALIFORNIA

2005

In the 1840s George Greene and his family were among squatters who homesteaded in the Outside Lands, a tract of sand dunes dotted with freshwater ponds beyond the western boundary of the city. After defying efforts to move them off, the Greenes eventually acquired a deed to their land, and over the decades planted thousands of eucalyptus, cypress, and pine to stabilize the sand. In 1892, George Jr. built the Trocadero Inn, a popular roadhouse under the trees. Over the years, despite pressures to sell as the city grew around them, the Greenes held on to their fourteen-acre property.

In 1928, John McLaren, superintendent of Golden Gate Park, took his friend Rosalie Meyer Stern, president of the Recreation Commission, to see the Greene property, which he was worried would be sold to developers. Stern was looking for a way to honor her late husband, and McLaren hoped she might find it in preserving the grove. "The stillness and quiet of the place made a deep impression" on her, and in

1931 Stern bought the property, dedicating it to the city to be used for free recreation and cultural events. The hollow was a natural amphitheater and had superb acoustics, a perfect setting for the "music, dramatics and pageantry" she envisioned.[1] The city subsequently acquired the adjacent land, including Pine Lake, creating a sixty-three-acre park, which has been the site of the annual Stern Grove Midsummer Music Festival since 1938. During the Depression, the Works Progress Administration constructed trails, rerouted a stream, and built walls along the entry roads and in the central area. But after sixty years the site was in need of renovation.

As the city's most renowned landscape architect, Halprin was the obvious choice for the redesign of this beloved community gathering place.[2] A small wooded valley Hal-

North terraces, 2013. Photograph by author.

Terraces from the stage, 2013. Photograph by author.

prin described as "canyon-like," the park comprises three
distinct sections: to the east, a winding drive downhill and
path through the forest; on the west, Pine Lake nestled in
the woods; and an adjoining meadow. In the center—surrounded by mature eucalyptus, redwood, and fir—is the
heart of the Grove, a space rich in local history. Now known
as the Rhoda Goldman Concert Meadow, it is where generations of audiences have picnicked on the grass, sat on the
wooded hillside, and listened to music.

At the Sloat Street entrance, Halprin installed a simple
stone gate with a metal treelike arch opening to the drive
that winds down into the Grove. An entry gate of stone
piers topped by a simple wooden lintel leads from a small
parking lot into the Grove, a grand clearing in the surrounding forest. Halprin's design is conceptually simple: a stage

Model, 2003. Courtesy LHC.

fronting a green meadow and a terraced stone amphitheater enclosed on all sides by a forest backdrop. Given the rectilinear shape of the space, Halprin's central design challenge was how to transform the grand semicircle of the classical Greek amphitheater into an elongated space. His solution was to straighten the arced stairs and terraces into long bands at the entrance.

Halprin expanded the stage area and supporting backstage offices tucked into the trees, framing the stage with another treelike arched metal structure. Ascending gradually from the turf meadow below the stage, low-rise steps with alternating rows of grass lead to larger terraces where stone predominates. The four-hundred-foot terraces are meticulously constructed as platforms, three tiers of stone thirty-six inches high interspersed with eighteen-inch seating walls. Stern Grove was constructed predominantly of a gray granite that has occasional reddish gold accents.[3] Each stone has been carefully cut and placed with the straight course of the upper blocks juxtaposed against a zigzag line of the stone face. Within these layers, seemingly random but individually

Detail of stone, 2013. Photograph by author.

placed uncut stones give the impression of having tumbled down the hillside. Perpendicular to the terraces, straight lines of steps cut across the grain of the Grove's contours, the warp and weft of a stone tapestry. Discrete yet overlapping sections of steps subtly subdivide the amphitheater. The upper stone terrace level merges into the forest, and ascending tiers of eight or ten logs for seating and backrests are set within the trees that frame views toward the stage.

Ensembles of vertical stones amid the terraces suggest a sculpture garden. Three stepped pyramidal islands rise up

Summer performance, 2014. Photograph by author.

from the lower terraces like ancient altars, creating small ziggurats that afford prime seating. The entire design feels simultaneously archaic and contemporary, as if an overgrown forested site had been discovered and then restored to a new use. A common first impression is that it resembles Machu Picchu, though Halprin never visited Peru. The debt to Greek theaters is clear, however. An office file labeled "Inspirations" features a site he knew well, the amphitheater on Mt. Tamalpais near his Kentfield home.

When he began working on the project, Halprin offered several community workshops, and the design was explored through a series of detailed models. Ultimately there were full-scale mock-ups of details, as he had made for the FDR Memorial. In some early versions the stone steps almost come up to the stage, but ultimately a grassed area was left between the elevated stage and seating.

Stern Grove can accommodate more than twelve thousand people at summer performances of music and dance. At other times the Grove is a site of celebrations, parties, and weddings. But most often it is a quiet refuge frequented by walkers. For children, the entire area is a vast play space. In the words of the landscape architect Linda Jewell, "Halprin has woven a magical landscape experience into the lives of thousands."[4]

Halprin had first visited the Grove in the 1950s to watch Anna dance. For the reopening in 2009, she choreographed the performance "Spirit of Place." In an inversion of the setting, on a rainy afternoon, the audience stood on the stage while the performers danced on the terraces among the stones. The ideas tested on the dance deck found expression a half century later at Stern Grove.

APPENDIX:
COMPARATIVE SCALE
DRAWINGS OF
SELECTED SITES

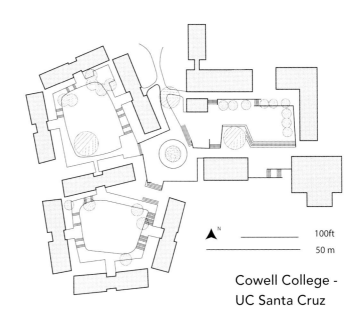

Cowell College - UC Santa Cruz

100ft
50 m

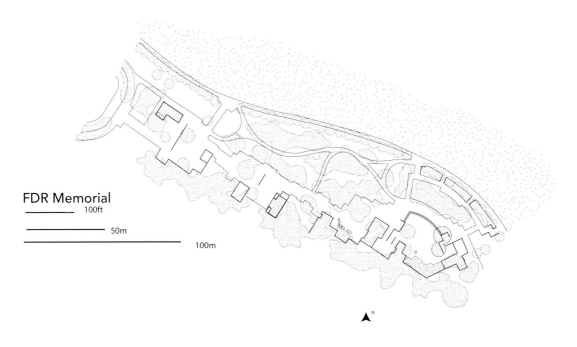

FDR Memorial

100ft
50m
100m

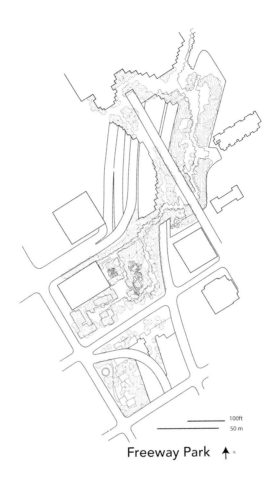

100ft
50 m

Freeway Park ↑ N

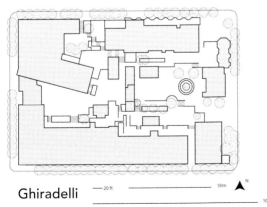

Ghiradelli
——20 ft ——————— 50m ▲ N
——————————————— 100m

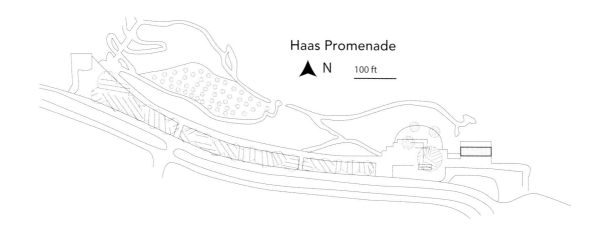

Haas Promenade

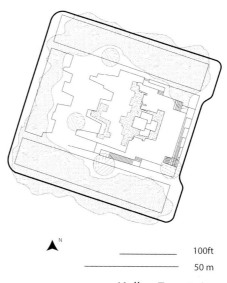

▲ N   ──── 100ft
       ──── 50 m

Keller Fountain

Levi Strauss Plaza

N 100 ft

Lovejoy Fountain

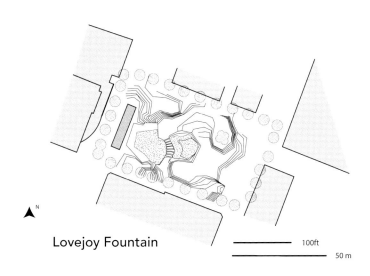

N

—————— 100ft
—————————— 50 m

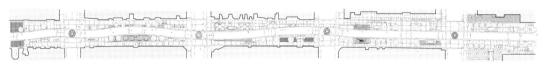

Nicollet Mall ▼   N ___100 ft___
4 blocks of the entire 11 block design

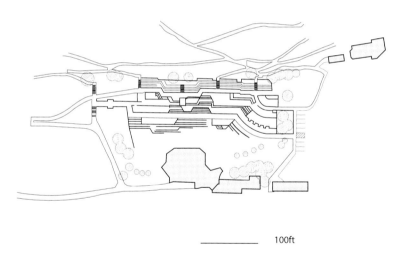

_____ 100ft

Stern Grove

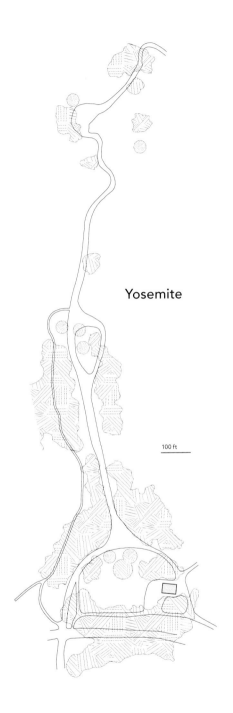

Yosemite

100 ft

NOTES

OVERVIEW

1. Judith R. Wasserman, "Dancing through Halprin's Portland," *Landscape Architecture* 99 (January 2009): 54–59.
2. Randy Gragg, ed., *Where the Revolution Began: Lawrence and Anna Halprin and the Reinvention of Public Space* (Washington, DC: Spacemaker Press, 2009), 76.
3. "Thoughts on Design," Notebook 2. Halprin numbered his 127 unpaginated notebooks, all but one of which are now held in the Lawrence Halprin Collection, Architectural Archives, University of Pennsylvania.
4. In a 1982 drawing he made when visiting burial caves in the Jezreel Valley, Halprin identifies a hillside where he planted trees a half century earlier.
5. Lawrence Halprin, *Cities* (New York: Reinhold, 1963), 7.
6. Lawrence Halprin, *Sketchbooks of Lawrence Halprin* (Tokyo: Process Architecture, 1981), 122.
7. The cabin burned down in 2001 and a new one was constructed on its foundation.
8. Lawrence Halprin, "The Gardens of the High Sierra," *Landscape* 11, no. 2 (Winter 1961–62): 26–28.
9. Lawrence Halprin, "The Shape of Erosion," *Landscape Architecture* 52 (January 1962): 87–88.
10. Notebook 7.

11. Lawrence Halprin, *A Life Spent Changing Places* (Philadelphia: University of Pennsylvania Press, 2011), 101. It is easy to see the link between the Sierra stone and water "gardens" and Halprin's subsequent fountain designs in Portland, Seattle, Denver, and Washington, DC.

12. Lawrence Halprin, *Notebooks, 1959–1971* (Cambridge: MIT Press, 1972), 295.

13. Lawrence Halprin, "Design as a Value System," *Places Journal* 6, no. 1 (1989): 62.

14. Rose Luria Halprin was president of Hadassah 1932–34 and 1947–52, momentous periods in Israel's history.

15. Elizabeth B. Kassler, *Modern Gardens and the Landscape* (New York: Museum of Modern Art, 1964).

16. Anna Halprin, interview by the author, July 24, 2013.

17. The landscape architects Geraldine Knight Scott and Burton Litton each designed one of the gardens; two lots were left undeveloped. Waverly Lowell, *Living Modern: A Biography of Greenwood Common* (Richmond, CA: William Stout, 2009).

18. Vignolo, who had worked part-time for Halprin in 1951 and 1952, became an associate in the firm in 1957.

19. The Weizmann Institute design was carried out by Lipa Yahalom and Dan Zur, who became the leading landscape architects of Israel's founding generation and were the first (and, as of this writing, only) members of their profession to receive the prestigious Israel Prize for architecture.

20. Kenneth Helphand, "Halprin in Israel," *Landscape Journal* 31, nos. 1–2 (2012): 199–217.

21. Halprin, *Notebooks*, 7.

22. Kathleen L. John-Alder, "A Field Guide to Form: Lawrence Halprin's Ecological Engagement with the Sea Ranch," *Landscape Journal* 31, nos. 1–2 (2012): 54.

23. Clare Cooper, "St. Francis Square: Attitudes of Its Residents," *AIA Journal* 56 (December 1971): 22–27.

24. Sproul has been characterized as "the plaza that changed the world." See http://californiahistoricalsociety.blogspot.com/2015/10/lawrence-halprin-and-plaza-that-changed.html.

25. Ada Louise Huxtable, "Coast Fountain Melds Art and Environment," *New York Times,* June 21, 1970.

26. Lawrence Halprin, *Freeways* (New York: Reinhold, 1966), 37.

27. The expansion of the Hadassah Hospital obliterated much of Halprin's design; the expansion of the Israel Museum (2010) retained major elements of his design and removed others.

28. Teddy Kolleck, "Re-Viewing Jerusalem," in *Lawrence Halprin: Changing Places,* exhibition catalog (San Francisco: San Francisco Museum of Modern Art, 1986), 84–113.

29. Notebook 38.
30. Aronson went on to design the Sherover and Trottner Promenades that completed the system.
31. Garrett Eckbo, *Public Landscape: Six Essays on Government and Environmental Design in the San Francisco Bay Area* (Berkeley: University of California, Institute of Governmental Studies, 1978), 28.
32. Halprin, *Notebooks,* 190.
33. For example, the architecture critic Allan Temko commented that the fountain looked as if it had been "deposited by a large concrete dog with square intestines." John King, "A Taste of Temko—His Take on 6 San Francisco Buildings," *San Francisco Chronicle,* May 1, 2009.
34. Halprin, *Cities,* 9.
35. Lawrence Halprin, *The RSVP Cycles: Creative Processes in the Human Environment* (New York: George Braziller, 1970), 1–2.
36. Halprin, *Notebooks,* 7–8.
37. See Alison Bick Hirsch, *City Choreographer: Lawrence Halprin in Urban Renewal America* (Minneapolis: University of Minnesota, 2014).
38. Kevin Lynch, *What Time Is This Place?* (Cambridge: MIT Press, 1972), 168.
39. Halprin, *RSVP Cycles,* 20.
40. John-Alder, "A Field Guide to Form," 67.
41. Halprin, *RSVP Cycles,* 4.
42. Notebook 2.
43. Notebook 5.
44. Lawrence Halprin & Associates brochure, 1970. Author's collection.
45. Lawrence Halprin and Jim Burns, *Taking Part: A Workshop Approach to Collective Creativity* (Cambridge: MIT Press, 1974).
46. On the park, see Ann Kumara, *Lawrence Halprin's Skyline Park* (New York: Princeton Architectural Press, 2012).
47. CHNMB became Nishita & Carter in 1985 before closing its doors in 1989.
48. In 2012 the Colorado firm Mundus Bishop sensitively completed, restored, and extended the design. Jane Margolis, "Star Witness," *Landscape Architecture* 105, no. 7 (July 2015): 84–103.
49. Halprin also received the AIA Medal for Allied Professionals in 1964, the American Society of Landscape Architects Medal in 1978, the Thomas Jefferson Foundation Medal in Architecture in 1979, the National Medal of Arts in 2002, the ASLA Design Medal in 2003, and the Michelangelo Award in 2005. He was elected to the National Academy of Design in 1987.
50. Others who worked in the office included workshop facilitator Jim Burns, landscape architects Brian Laczko and Gary Roth, and slide librarian Jeri Sully.
51. Halprin, "Notes of my remarks . . . on the occasion of Mother's Memo-

rial Service in Jerusalem & the unveiling of her grave," December 24, 1978. Notebook 61.

52. "Lawrence Halprin Projects: Donnell Garden," interview by Charles A. Birnbaum, *Pioneers of American Landscape Design: Oral History Project,* Cultural Landscape Foundation, March 2003, http://tclf.org/pioneer /oral-history/lawrence-halprin.

53. Laurie D. Olin, "An American Original: On the Landscape Architecture Career of Lawrence Halprin," *Studies in the History of Gardens & Designed Landscapes: An International Quarterly* 32, no. 3 (2012): 162.

54. Peter Walker and Melanie Simo, *Invisible Gardens: The Search for Modernism in the American Landscape* (Cambridge: MIT Press, 1994), 145.

55. "Lawrence Halprin Projects."

56. Anna Halprin interview.

57. Skyline Park in Denver was destroyed; Hadassah Hospital and the Israel Museum were radically remodeled.

CAYGILL GARDEN

1. Joseph E. Howland, "The Garden of the Next America Is an Outdoor Room," *House Beautiful,* April 1953, 148–49; "Let's Invite Everybody In," *House and Home,* June 1953.

2. "Notes on the Caygill Garden," January, 22, 1952, 014.II.A.024, Lawrence Halprin Collection, Architectural Archives, University of Pennsylvania.

3. The influence of modern artists was a basic tenet of landscape modernism and was dramatically manifested in the work of Bay Area designers.

4. "Notes on the Caygill Garden."

HALPRIN DANCE DECK

1. Lawrence Halprin, *A Life Spent Changing Places* (Philadelphia: University of Pennsylvania Press, 2011), 75.

2. Lawrence Halprin and Anna Halprin, "Dance Deck in the Woods," *Impulse: The Annual of Contemporary Dance* 50, no. 1 (1956): 24.

OLD ORCHARD SHOPPING CENTER

1. Peter Walker, "Lawrence Halprin & Associates, 1954: A Brief Memoir," *Landscape Journal* 31, no. 1/2 (2012): 29.

2. Philip M. Klutznick with Sidney Hyman, *Angles of Vision: A Memoir of My Lives* (Chicago: Ivan R. Dee, 1991), 190.

3. Jerrold Loebl to Halprin, 1956, 014.I.A.1472–1482, Lawrence Halprin Collection, Architectural Archives, University of Pennsylvania.

4. "Garden Setting Lends Charm to Chicago's Newest Shopping Center," *Architectural Record* 122, no. 3 (September 1957): 220–27.

5. James Hornbeck, "Shopping Can Be a Pleasure," *Architectural Record* 122, no. 3 (September 1957): 205.

SEA RANCH

1. Lawrence Halprin, *The RSVP Cycles* (New York: George Braziller 1969) 98.

2. Lawrence Halprin, *Sea Ranch . . . Diary of an Idea* (Sea Ranch: Comet Studios, 1995), 7

3. Donlyn Lyndon and Jim Alinder, *The Sea Ranch* (New York: Princeton Architectural Press, 2014). 39.

4. Notebook 65.

5. Kathleen L. John-Alder, "A Field Guide to Form: Lawrence Halprin's Ecological Engagement with Sea Ranch," *Landscape Journal* 31, nos. 1–2 (2012): 69.

NICOLLET MALL

1. William Severini Kowinski, *The Malling of America: An Inside Look at the Great Consumer Paradise* (New York: William Morrow, 1985).

GHIRARDELLI SQUARE

1. Jane Holtz Kay, "Rouse-ification of Lower Manhattan," *Christian Science Monitor,* September 16, 1983.

2. Howard Malchow, *Special Relations: The Americanization of Britain* (Stanford: Stanford University Press, 2011), 265.

UNIVERSITY OF CALIFORNIA, SANTA CRUZ

1. Paul V. Turner, *Campus: An American Planning Tradition* (Cambridge: MIT Press, 1984), 282.

2. Quoted in Garrett Eckbo, *Public Landscape: Six Essays on Government and Environmental Design in the San Francisco Bay Area* (Berkeley: Berkeley Institute of Governmental Studies, University of California, 1978), 78.

PORTLAND OPEN SPACE SEQUENCE

1. Lawrence Halprin, "The Gardens of the High Sierra," *Landscape* 11 (Winter 1961–62): 26–28.

2. It is impossible to note all the contributors to projects. CMS Col-

laborative, founded by Dick Shay, were consultants on his fountain projects, however.

3. Lawrence Halprin, *Cities* (New York: Reinhold, 1963), 134. In the revised second edition the fountains are featured along with Ghirardelli Square, Nicollet Avenue, and Embarcadero Plaza, all works where he had the opportunity to put his theories and ideas into practice.

4. Halprin quoted in *Process: Architecture, No. 4: Lawrence Halprin,* ed. Ching-Yu Chang (Tokyo: Process Architecture Publishing, 1978), 167; Ada Louise Huxtable, "Coast Fountain Melds Art and Environment," *New York Times,* June 21, 1970.

5. Huxtable, "Coast Fountain."

FREEWAY PARK

1. Subsequently, a movement to cover the freeway led by Victor Steinbrueck, a professor of architecture at the University of Washington, set the stage for Halprin's work.

2. John Pastier, "Evaluation: Park Atop a Freeway," *AIA Journal* 72 (June 1983): 43.

3. Sally Woodbridge, "Green Lid for I-5," *Progressive Architecture* 58, no. 6 (June 1977): 86.

THE WILLAMETTE VALLEY: CHOICES FOR THE FUTURE

1. The idea of the Pacific Northwest as an ecotopia was dramatically crystallized in Ernest Callenbach's 1975 novel, *Ecotopia.*

2. Randy Gragg, " A Designer Who Changed Portland, and Oregon, Forever," *Oregonian,* April 5, 2006.

3. While visionary, the report was a pragmatic document, and the need for a comprehensive land use planning process to put theory into practice was a central concern. The Land Conservation and Development Commission was established in 1973 to work with local communities in meeting a set of fourteen statewide goals. In the intervening years the role of the Councils of Government has expanded, and since 1979, Metro, the elected regional government, serves almost half the state's population around Portland. David Hulse, coauthor of *The Willamette River Basin Planning Atlas: Trajectories of Environmental and Ecological Change* (2002), lauds the report's innovative methodological legacy offering a lesson on how to use scenarios as a way to imagine the future employing data as the basis for projecting a spatial narrative.

4. Over the years the Halprin office engaged in many large-scale planning and design projects and reports for agencies and cities including Everett, Washington; Charlottesville, Virginia; New York City; and projects for the Virgin Islands and the Navajo Nation. Often shelved

for political reasons, these reports offer insights and ideas, directions for the future, which we can hope will be returned to, much as plans done by the Olmsted office a century ago have been and, updated, proven viable in the modern era.

FRANKLIN DELANO ROOSEVELT MEMORIAL

1. The first competition in 1959 had 574 submissions; the second, in 1966 was by invitation, with 55 entries. The Yamasaki Halprin plan was not among the finalists.
2. Lawrence Halprin, *The Franklin Delano Roosevelt Memorial* (San Francisco: Chronicle Books, 1997), 7.
3. Ibid., 31.
4. I am indebted to Laurie Olin for this observation.
5. Laurie Olin, "The FDR Memorial Wheelchair Controversy and a 'Taking Part' Workshop Experience," *Landscape Journal* 31, nos. 1–2 (2012) 183–97.

LEVI STRAUSS PLAZA

1. In one early alternative, the park was a large pond with a circumnavigating path and an island; in another, water was entirely eliminated from the park.

THE HAAS PROMENADE AND THE RICHARD AND RHODA GOLDMAN PROMENADE

1. Notebook 65.
2. Bruce Levin, "Memories of Working with Lawrence Halprin," lecture at Technion, Israeli Institute of Technology, Haifa, April 2011, transcript, collection of the author.
3. Bruce Levin, June 23, 2011, e-mail to author.

YOSEMITE

1. Frederick Law Olmsted, *The Papers of Frederick Law Olmsted,* vol. 5, *The California Frontier, 1863–1865,* ed. Victoria Post Ranney (Baltimore: Johns Hopkins University Press, 1990). 500.
2. Ibid., 490.
3. Carl Nolte, "Yosemite: Finishing Touch on Nature/New Paths, Markers Highlight Waterfalls, Former Indian Village," *SF Gate,* April 5, 2005.
4. The group was previously called the Yosemite Fund; it is the largest nonprofit Yosemite "friends" group.

5. The CCC did extensive design and construction work in both national and state parks throughout the country.
6. Halprin quoted in Erik Skindrud, "Yosemite Falls: Where Nature Meets the Crowd," LandscapeOnline.com, July 2005.

SIGMUND STERN RECREATION GROVE

1. *Nature's Music Box: Fifty Seasons of the Stern Grove Midsummer Music Festival, 1938–1937* (San Francisco: Stern Grove Festival Association, 1987).
2. A study by Royston Hanamoto Alley & Abey had evaluated the site, and a forest management plan by HortScience advised selective thinning.
3. The stone for the project was quarried in China.
4. Linda Jewell, "The Spirit of Stone," *Landscape Architecture* 96 (February 2006): 87.

INDEX

Maguire Gardens (Los Angeles), 53, *53*

Manhattan Square Park (Rochester, NY), 59, *59*

Mansfeld, Al (architect), and Israel Museum, 34

Marcus, Clare Cooper (environmental psychologist), on St. Francis Square, 29

Marin General Hospital (Novato), 17–18

Market Street (San Francisco), 35, *36, 40*

Marquis, Robert (architect), and St. Francis Square, 28

McCall, Tom (OR governor), 39; and Project Foresight, 149–50

McCulley, Byron, and CHNMB Associates, 49

McHarg, Ian (landscape architect), and environmental design, 6, 95, 97

McIntyre garden (Hillsborough, CA), 18; central role of water, 25

Minneapolis, MN: *Hennepin Avenue Report,* 38; Nicollet Mall, 26, 40, 99–107

modern artists, influence on landscape modernism, 65, 222n3

Modern Gardens and the Landscape (Museum of Modern Art), Halprin's work in, 19

Moore, Charles, 91, 92; collaboration with Halprin, 9, 24–25, 52, 92, 133; fascination with water, 133

Moore Ruble Yudell (architects), and Halprin cabin, 92

"motation," 40, 75, *98,* 105, 106, 192

Mountain Home Studio (Kentfield), 75. *See also* Halprin dance deck

Mullen, Dee (Halprin office manager), 50

Mundus Bishop (landscape architects), and Babi Yar Memorial Park, 221n48

National Register of Historic Places, Halprin projects listed, 59, 117, 137

Navaho Nation, Halprin projects for, 224–25n4

New York City: childhood in, 6, 12; projects in, 25, 59, 224–25n4

New York City Department of Housing and Urban Development, 37–38

New York New York (Lawrence Halprin & Associates), 37–39

Nicholson, Simon (landscape architect), in Halprin firm, 57

Nicollet Avenue (Minneapolis, MN): in *Cities,* 224n3; heart of commercial district, 101; redesign of, 26

Nicollet Mall (Minneapolis, MN) 26, 40, 99, *100, 102, 103, 104, 105;* importance of design and streetscape elements, 40, 101, *106;* nation's first transit mall, 26, 101, 107; redesign and revitalization of, 107; serpentine configuration, 26, 101; study model, *27;* use of motation in design, 40, *98,* 105–6

Nishita, Satoru (landscape architect): and CHNMB Associates, 49, 221n47; collaboration on Babi Yar Memorial Park, 50; in Halprin firm, 21

Noguchi, Isamu (landscape architect): and Jerusalem

Sproul Plaza (Berkeley, CA), 30, *30,* 31

Steinbrueck, Victor (architect), and covering Seattle freeway, 224n1

Stern, Rosalie Meyer, 203. *See also* Sigmund Stern Recreation Grove

Stern Grove. *See* Sigmund Stern Recreation Grove

Stern Grove Midsummer Music Festival, 204

Stevenson College (UCSC), 120; knoll, 125, *125. See also* University of California, Santa Cruz

St. Francis Square (San Francisco), 28–30

Stoller, Claude (architect), and St. Francis Square, 28

"Street Life Project" (Whyte), 6

Streets for People (Rudofsky), 6

Sully, Jeri (Halprin slide librarian), 221n50

Sunset magazine, 16; work on cover, 18

"Take Part" process: collaboration with Anna Halprin on, 75; method of engaging public, 47; at Yosemite, 192. *See also* Halprin, Lawrence: personal views and characteristics: social activism; RSVP cycles; workshops

Taking Part: A Workshop Approach to Collective Creativity (Halprin and Burns), 47

Taliesin (Wright studio), Halprin visit to, 13

Tamalpa Institute, 75. *See also* Halprin dance deck

Tayelet (Jerusalem), 35, 180; as performance, 187–88

Temko, Allan (architecture critic), on Embarcadero Fountain, 221n33

Thiel, Philip (architect), and notation systems, 40

Thiry, Paul (architect), proposal for Seattle freeway, 141

Thompson, Benjamin (architect), and "festival marketplaces," 110. *See also* Benjamin Thompson & Associates

Trottner Park (Jerusalem), 180. *See also* Trottner Promenade

Trottner Promenade (Jerusalem), 184, 221n30. *See also* Trottner Park

Tunnard, Christopher (landscape architect), *Gardens in the Modern Landscape,* 14, 175–76

Turnbull, William (architect): and Lovejoy Plaza, 133; and Sea Ranch, 91, 92

United Nations Headquarters (Jerusalem), 179, 184

University of California, Berkeley, 17, 30, 57; campus plan, 22; graduates in Halprin firm, 21, 23, 24; Sproul Plaza design, 30–31

University of California, Davis, Master Plan, 21

University of California, Santa Cruz (UCSC), 121, 126; clustering of colleges, 119, 120; courtyards, 120, 122, 123, 127; distinct design of each college, 120; Halprin's highlighting of natural beauty, 31; importance of trees, 31, 119, 120, 122, 123, *123,* 125; master plan, 31, *118,* 119, 120; meadows, 119, 122, 124; pedestrian paths, 118, 120

University of Wisconsin–Madison, 13

urban renewal projects, 6, 15, 35,